"Well written, insigl
Thanks."
— C

"Mr. Bair, I really, really enjoyed reading your answer! Thank you for taking the time to explain some very important questions that some folks have concerning the word of God. It's my prayer that your answer will help erase doubts that some people may have had. Satan is trying His best to plant all the doubt he can into people's hearts, your answer may very well help save some doubting souls that would have otherwise been lost! Thanks again and God Bless!"
— James Henderson[2]

"Excellent, well-written and comprehensive [...]
There were so many who suffered (and still suffer, today) martyrdom for the Risen Christ. They would not do so if it had been a lie."
— Janice Mermikli[3]

"Goodness gracious. The amount of commitment you've given to these comments is incredible. I respect your opinions thoroughly... you've definitely spent lots of time reviewing how your faith interlocks with its evidences. And I can also certainly see how the archaeological evidence supports your beliefs, thus strengthening them."
— Daniel Lamping[4]

Hope You're Curious
Real Answers to Honest Questions

Kyle Davison Bair

Copyright © 2020 by Kyle Davison Bair
All rights reserved. No part of this book may be reproduced, scanned, or distributed in any printed or electronic form without permission.
First Edition: January 2020
Second Edition: February 2020
ISBN: 9798612390183
Printed in the United States of America

Scripture quotations marked NIV are from The Holy Bible, New International Version. Copyright © 1973, 1978, 1984, International Bible Society.

Scripture quotations marked ESV are from The Holy Bible, English Standard Version® (ESV®). Copyright © 2001 by Crossway, a publishing ministry of Good News Publishers.

Scripture quotations marked NET are from The NET Bible® Copyright ® 2005 by Biblical Studies Press, LLC.

Scripture quotations marked NLT are from The Holy Bible, New Living Translation. Copyright ® 1996, 2004, 2015 by Tyndale House Foundation.

Scripture quotations marked MSG are from The Message: The Bible in Contemporary Language. Copyright ®2002 by Eugene H. Peterson.

All emphasis added to the Scripture quotations is the author's.

To My Grandma.

You've loved us so well for as long as I can remember. You always make us feel special. I see the light of God's love shining through you.

Want free books?

I put together a collection of stories, articles, and books to give away to everyone who joins me on this journey.

To grab your copies, visit www.kyledavisonbair.com.

I write constantly, from popular sites like Quora.com or Medium.com, to Christian publications like PRAY Magazine or the EFCA Blog, to short story hubs like Daily Science Fiction. I have several books in the works, from novels to apologetics to how you can persuade audiences as effectively as Jesus did. I also speak at various events and host the audio/video whenever I can. The best way for you to keep up with it all is the site above.

I also love to give away free stuff, both the stuff I've worked on and the stuff that others are giving away free. I'll keep you updated.

It'll be fascinating – as long as you're curious.

Table of Contents

Introduction xi
1. Which religion is the true religion and why? 1
2. Do you believe that the Tree of Knowledge of Good and Evil was meant to be eaten from? 8
3. If God existed then X, and if God didn't exist then Y. What do you think are X and Y? 14
4. When will the star of Bethlehem be visible again? 18
5. The shepherd is a prominent, meaningful metaphor in the Bible. But why do the prophets ask us to think of Messiah as our Good Shepherd? 29
6. What is the hardest thing to believe in the Bible? .32
7. Is it true that many Christians believe that both heaven and hell are a state of mind rather than an actual place? 33
8. Why and how should I read the Bible? 35
9. Can anyone explain the Trinity in simple language? 38
10. How do I grow my faith in Christianity? 43
11. Unlike other failed Messiahs, why did Jesus' message endure after his death? 49
12. Do you find it incomprehensible that despite the track record of science in improving people's lives, evangelicals will still give greater credence to blind

acceptance of Scripture?..54

13. What parts of the New Testament have been significantly edited?..71

14. What is the origin of the idea of a loving God?.....73

15. Why were the four canonical gospels written so long after Christ's death and resurrection?..............78

16. Isn't it unfair to Jesus that the three main branches of Christianity claim to derive their divine mandate from Him as God, although He said: 'Why callest thou me good, none is good except the Father'?...89

17. Why was God mad at Adam and Eve for eating the apple and becoming knowledgeable?....................96

18. How does the Christian belief in the resurrection provide a resource for dealing with and understanding suffering?..98

19. Was there an eclipse when Jesus was crucified?.101

20. Why do I think thoughts that I'm opposed to thinking? Could the devil be speaking deceptive messages to me?..109

21. How do we know how the apostles died? Is there evidence?..113

22. Do the majority of Christians believe that you can't be a good person without being a Christian?.......120

23. Why do the Gospels differ in Jesus' response to the High Priest when asked if he is the Messiah? He either answers cryptically or in the affirmative. ..121

24. Do you agree with Sarah Sanders' belief that God wanted Trump to be president? Why do you think this is so?..136

25. Do Christians mind being friends with people who hate everything about Christianity? 142
26. What would Jesus say about Christianity today? 144
27. What are some of the best ways to express "I love you" without actually saying it? 148
28. Is Jesus Christ the Son of God or God? 152
29. What evidence is there for Jesus Christ's death, burial, and resurrection? 157
30. Does God kill people He hates by diseases and accidents? 164
31. How would a skilled magician perform some of the alleged miracles of Jesus, only using the technology available at the time? 165
32. Why are the Greek gods considered myths while the Christian God isn't? 172
33. Do you ever speculate about the details of Jesus' childhood? 180
34. What are the biblical justifications for racial segregation? 186
35. Is there any archaeological proof that Jesus existed? 189
36. What, exactly, is your basis for believing that the Bible is true; not necessarily the word of God, but true? 198
37. What is the root cause of enmity between Islam, Christianity and Judaism? 201
38. Is it accurate to say that humankind is "wired to worship"? Why is this the case and what does this mean? 203

ix

39. Why did God allow sin to enter this world? 206

40. Why is Jesus named Jesus? 210

41. Do Christians and Jews know that we Muslims regard David & Jesus as equal with the Prophet Muhammad as prophets and messengers of God to mankind? 212

42. How do you know that Jesus is merciful? 216

43. If Jesus had married and procreated children, could those children have sinned at any time? 217

44. How are religions true? 219

45. If in the Holy Bible there are contradictions that cannot be explained, what are they, and why are their explanations invalid? 221

46. Why is Esther in the Bible when it doesn't mention God? 235

47. How did slave owners justify slavery using the Bible? 237

48. If God made it easy to believe in Him, would everyone do it? 241

Afterward 243

Introduction

Where do you find answers to your deepest questions?

For better or worse, the Internet makes us bold. People say things they wouldn't say face-to-face – sometimes for good, many times not.

People also ask things they wouldn't in person, or feel they can't ask. Sadly, many churches shun those who ask hard questions.

But this is not the way God made us. **Asking good questions is one of the most sacred things you can ever do.**

Many Christians flock to public forums to ask the deep questions of faith they haven't found answers for anywhere else:

- *How can anyone explain the Trinity in simple language? I have been struggling with it for over 20 years and no priest was able to give a convincing explanation.*

- *What would Jesus say about Christianity today?*

- *How do I grow my faith in Christianity? I'm still young and have big dreams and aspirations, but want to achieve them the right way, in God's word.*

- *Why did Jesus call Himself the Son of God instead of just calling Himself God?*

Alongside Christians seeking answers arise scores of challenges to Christianity. Skeptics pelt Christianity with questions of all kinds, trying to attack or shame or undermine the religion they reject:

- *Why is the Holy Bible full of contradictions?*

- *Is there any archaeological proof that Jesus existed?*

- *How did slave owners justify slavery using the Bible?*

- *Why do Christians insist on blind acceptance of Scripture when science has such a great track record of improving people's lives?*

In the unique way God made me, these questions excite me. It doesn't matter how exhausted I am. When I see a question like this, adrenaline shoots through my veins, my mind ramps into high gear, and I dive in.

This book includes four dozen answers I've had the privilege of writing over the past two years. At the time of publication, these answers have already been read over 300,000 times, and the rate of new readers discovering them is steadily increasing.

This was such a fun book to write! I love interacting with those who have genuine questions. There's no speculation about whether these topics are relevant. These are things people want to know — and in many cases, *need* to know.

These are conversations I love having. It's a thrill to include so many in this book for you to enjoy, as well.

God receives all the glory for everything in this book. He does not leave me on my own as I write. If I were to share my own opinions to each of these questions, there'd be no reason to read them.

But God provides wisdom to all who ask. In each answer, I strive to communicate the wisdom of God from the Scriptures, empowered by His Spirit. I ask God to give me His words for the people asking these questions, so that they encounter Him in these answers.

Jesus is the Truth. He is more than wise, more than smart, more than well-educated, more than clever. He is Truth embodied. In every answer, I pray that you will see Jesus in His truth, and that you will draw nearer to Him.

God is not afraid of questions. He delights in them, as He never lacks the answer. An honest question asked of God always leads us closer to Him, if we're willing to hear the answer.

I hope you're curious.

Question 1

Which religion is the true religion and why?[5]

This could be a complicated question. But it isn't.

Let's take it in pieces: *Which religion is the true religion?*

Answer: **Christianity**.

Now for the big one: *Why?*

Answer: **Because Jesus is alive.**

If Jesus is alive, then there is no more important fact in all of human history.

If Jesus is alive, then we have definitive proof of God doing what only God could do.

If Jesus is alive, then we have all the proof we need that what He said about Himself is true. Anyone can claim to be God. Anyone can claim to be the only true representative of God. But no one can defeat death. No one but God.

This is why the Christian church has been shouting Jesus' Resurrection from the very beginning:

> Now I want to make clear for you, brothers and sisters, the gospel that I preached to you, that you received and on which you stand, and by which you are being saved, if you hold firmly to the message I preached to you—unless you believed in vain. For I passed on to you as of first importance what I also received—that **Christ died** for our sins according to the scriptures, and that **he was buried**, and that **he was raised on the third day according to the Scriptures**. (1 Corinthians 15:1–4 NET)

This is one of the earliest of all documents ever written in the history of Christianity. Not only does it talk about Jesus being alive, but it makes clear that Jesus' Resurrected life is the central fact of Christianity. Without it — if Jesus is dead — then there is no Christianity:

> Now if Christ is being preached as raised from the dead, how can some of you say there is no resurrection of the dead? But if there is no resurrection of the dead, then not even Christ has been raised. And **if Christ has not been raised, then our preaching is futile and your faith is empty**. Also, we are found to be false witnesses about God, because we have testified against God that he raised Christ from the dead, when in reality he did not raise him, if indeed the dead are not raised. For if the dead are not raised, then not even Christ has been raised. And **if Christ has not been raised, your faith is useless; you are still in your sins**. Furthermore, those who have fallen asleep in Christ have also perished. For if only in this life we

have hope in Christ, we should be pitied more than anyone. But **now Christ has been raised from the dead, the firstfruits of those who have fallen asleep**. (1 Corinthians 15:12–20 NET)

Christianity began for one reason: Jesus died on a Cross, was buried, and came back to life.

This is no legendary story that grew over time. From the earliest we can trace back, the central tenet of Christianity is that Jesus claimed to be God and Jesus defeated death, proving it.

But here you may push back. After all, you can't just tell people that Jesus came back from death. You have to prove it! This is an extraordinary claim. It requires extraordinary evidence.

Precisely so. For this reason, Paul backs up his claims by pointing his readers to hundreds upon hundreds of eye-witnesses they can go check with to verify everything Paul is saying:

> [After His Resurrection, Jesus] appeared to **Cephas**, then to the **Twelve**. Then he appeared to **more than five hundred** of the brothers and sisters at one time, most of whom are still alive, though some have fallen asleep. Then he appeared to **James**, then to **all the apostles**. Last of all, as though to one born at the wrong time, **he appeared to me also**. (1 Corinthians 15:5–8 NET)

Christianity was still a small world at this time. These eye-witnesses were easy to find.

This is how you know Paul was telling the truth: he emphasized "Don't believe my words. Go and check for yourselves."

Christianity thrived on the attitude of "go and check for yourselves." Any seeker could explore Jesus' life thoroughly, because **every major event in Jesus' life happened publicly**.

If anyone doubted whether Jesus truly fed a crowd of 5,000 miraculously, or whether Jesus took control of the Temple after riding into Jerusalem triumphantly, or whether Jesus was publicly executed, or whether Jesus' tomb was empty, all they had to do was visit Israel and ask around. Eye-witnesses abounded.

Further, **the Gospel writers published their records of Jesus' life in the lands where the events happened while the eye-witnesses were still alive.**

Even the most skeptical scholars will agree that Matthew, Mark, and Luke were published and distributed in the land during the lifetime of those who saw Jesus personally.

Yet despite having enemies at every corner, *no one ever charged the Gospels with inaccuracy.*

Think about that. Consider the story of Jesus feeding a crowd of over 5,000 people by miraculous multiplying a few loaves and a few fish. It happened at a specific place on the shore of the Sea of Galilee in a specific year. All four Gospels record the event.

If this event never happened, then no one in these communities would ever believe in Jesus. They would know instantly that this book was bogus for claiming that such a life-altering event happened in their region, yet mysteriously no one knows about it. If this had been the situation, Christianity would never have exploded in this region.

Consider instead what actually happened:

All four Gospels record that Jesus fed over 5,000 people by a clear and undeniable miracle. When these accounts are published and circulated, the people living in the region did not challenge the accounts one bit. There is not a single record of anyone calling the Gospels liars or even exaggerators! Even the fiercest enemies of Christianity at the time could not attack the Gospels on the basis of inaccuracy.

That's stunning. And it's extraordinary.

In terms of evidence, it's conclusive. The Gospels seem to record outlandish, impossible events. **But if the people who witnessed them confirmed them, and if Christianity's enemies couldn't put the lie to anything the Gospels record, then all the evidence is lining up to corroborate the Gospel's claims.**

The long and short of it is this: **Jesus lived in history**. You could go back and check the stories. As outlandish as Jesus' claims seem to be, no one in the early church asked their audience for blind faith. Instead they kept asking their audience to go and check.

This is why Christianity exploded so quickly in the first century. The evidence was absolutely extraordinary. Jesus said He was God and did what only God could do in order to prove it.

Christianity exploded because its claims were true — and they could be checked. This was no minor cult that needed to isolate its followers to indoctrinate them. This was a public movement that encouraged its followers to constantly check its claims. They did. That's why they believed.

> "The evidence of our Lord's life and death and resurrection, may be, and often has been shown to be, satisfactory; **it is good according to the common rules for distinguishing good evidence from bad**. Thousands and ten thousands of persons have gone through it piece by piece, as carefully as ever judge summed up on a most important cause: I have myself done it many times over, not to persuade others, but to satisfy myself. I have been used for many years to study the histories of other times, and to examine and weigh the evidence of those who have written about them, and **I know of no one fact in the history of mankind which is proved by better and fuller evidence of every**

sort, to the understanding of a fair inquirer, than the great sign which God hath given us that **Christ died and rose again from the dead.**"[6]

> — *Thomas Arnold, Professor of History, Oxford*

Question 2

Do you believe that the Tree of Knowledge of Good and Evil was meant to be eaten from? Do you feel that perhaps a certain time would have to pass (gaining experience) as sinners before God would allow the tree to be eaten from?[7]

This question highlights how amazing God is.

Some speculate that the Tree of the Knowledge of Good and Evil makes God out to be cruel, as though God is punishing Adam and Eve for doing what He knows they'll do, anyway. Others speculate that the Tree refers to hidden knowledge, or depicts a metaphorical falling away from moral perfection.

But it's none of those things.

Everything about creation — including Eden and its two most significant trees — displays how amazingly good God really is.

Let me explain.

Part one: ***Do you believe that the Tree of Knowledge of Good and Evil was meant to be eaten from?***

Simple answer: **No.**

God is clear that Adam and Eve are to avoid the Tree of the Knowledge of Good and Evil entirely:

> "You may surely eat of every tree of the garden, but of the Tree of the Knowledge of Good and Evil you shall not eat, for in the day that you eat of it you shall surely die." (Genesis 2:17–28)

God is clear about *why* they need to avoid it: if they eat it, they will die.

God is also clear that there's *no need* to eat from it. He provides them with an abundance of food, with every other plant available to feast from.

God draws a clear boundary to *protect* His children. He also provides abundantly in every conceivable way, so they feel no need to cross that boundary.

And here's the part most people miss: **Adam and Eve didn't *want* to eat from the Tree of Knowledge of Good and Evil.**

How do we know this? Read the text. After God creates Adam and Eve and furnishes a literal Paradise for them, they are having the time of their lives. They live contentedly in the Garden, eating its fruit, enjoying life with God and with each other.

The forbidden tree doesn't tempt them in the slightest.

Adam and Eve don't agonize with each other, wondering if they should eat the forbidden fruit. Genesis 2 ends with them perfectly content, naked and without shame. **They simply didn't care about the forbidden tree.**

God didn't set them up for failure. They succeeded just fine in their challenge. They had no interest in the forbidden tree until the serpent explicitly drew their attention to it.

To wrap this up: No, God did not mean for Adam and Eve to eat from the Tree, and Adam and Eve had no desire to eat from it, themselves.

Part two: *Do you feel that perhaps a certain time would have to pass (gaining experience) as sinners before God would allow the tree to be eaten from?*

It's an interesting question, but it gets the details backwards.

Look at the name: the Tree of the Knowledge of Good AND Evil.

Before eating from it, Adam and Eve knew only good. They did not sin, they had no experience with sin, and thus could gain no experience as sinners without eating from the Tree.

Eating from the Tree spoiled Adam and Eve. They went from a thorough knowledge of everything *good* to a corrupted knowledge of things good *and* evil. They took a glass full of good, pure water and filled it with half water, half poison.

Think about everything *good* in life: love, joy, peace, unity, beauty, satisfaction, intimacy, purpose, destiny, provision, safety, knowledge, comfort, health. Adam and Eve had these in abundance. God delighted to provide these without limit.

But once they ate, they gained knowledge of everything evil: division, blame, guilt, shame, accusation, lying, fear, hiding, corruption, death, loss, sickness, pain, sadness.

God wasn't waiting for a certain time to pass before poisoning His children with these things. **God wanted to keep His children full of the knowledge of good — and good alone.** That's the endpoint that God restores the world back to, according to the book of Revelation.

Eating from the Tree had no benefit. It had no upside. It was not a secret test to add wisdom, or next-level knowledge to access only after gaining enough experience. There was nothing good about replacing pure water with poison.

Eating from the Tree was a tragedy of the greatest magnitude.

And so we come back to the beginning: **all of this reveals how good God is.**

Look at all the ways God could have done this differently, and how each one contains a different form of failure:

1. God could have given no warning and no boundaries. Adam and Eve could have stumbled into the worst decision of their lives with knowledge to avoid it.

2. God could have given no choice. He could have created Adam and Eve to be like Him, possessing minds and wills and creativity, yet have no option to make a meaningful choice. That's intellectual slavery: ability with no opportunity.

3. God could have given no mental ability. He could have made a planet of animals alone, with no creature possessing higher thought or decision-making ability. It would be a nice zoo, but it would not accomplish God's desire of children — beings made in His image, as babies are made in the image of their parents.

4. God could have stopped Adam and Eve, forcing their hands away from the Tree. This would have violated their authority to make their own decisions, which was one of the first gifts God gave: *"And let them have dominion..."* (Genesis 1:26). Authority is no authority if you can only use it to take approved actions.

5. God could have abandoned Adam and Eve after they ate. Yet He stayed with them. He had a

continual, daily relationship with them and their children for hundreds of years after they ate. God stuck with His children.

If God wanted children — beings with minds and wills and creativity, as He had; beings who could choose to love freely, as He could — **then this was the only way.**

God gave them minds. God gave them clear boundaries. God gave them clear warnings, telling them exactly what would happen. God gave them the freedom to make their own choice. God gave them the authority to carry out their own choice and experience its consequences. And God stayed with them, loving them regardless of what they chose.

That is why God is so amazingly, unbelievably good.

Question 3

If God existed then X, and if God didn't exist then Y. What do you think are X and Y?[8]

If God existed... then something else can exist.

If God does not exist... then nothing else can exist.

Some might think this is too bold. How can you tie existence to God?

Because logic demands it.

Take any created thing in all existence — anything that began to exist. You could take planet Earth, the universe itself, your iPhone, or an idea hatching in your mind right now.

Then ask one simple question: where did that come from? It always came from something existing prior. So now shift your focus to that and ask the same question: where did *that* come from?

No matter where you start, this chain of questions always leads you back to one inescapable conclusion: everything that began to exist had to originate with something that did not.

Not convinced? Let's take planet Earth as our example. Where did Earth come from? It came from a cloud of interstellar gas and dust that formed the solar system. Where did that cloud of gas and dust come from? It came from the Big Bang. Where did that come from? It had to come from something that existed before it.

But the Big Bang seems to be the beginning of our universe. What could come before the beginning?

The only logical answer is something that has always existed.

And that's one of the essential qualities of God.

At this point, some may object and ask, "Why can't the universe be eternal? Why appeal to God?"

It's a good question, but the answer is clear: **because the universe isn't eternal.** We've been studying our universe endlessly. We still haven't found a single eternal quality. Everything about our universe is finite: it exists with limited space, energy, time, and capability. There's nothing eternal about our universe.

So we arrive back at the beginning.

If God exists, then something else can exist. Or to expand it: if a Being exists who has no beginning, but has always existed, then this Being can create new things that have beginnings.

On the other hand, if God does not exist, then nothing can exist. Or to expand it: if there is no Being who always existed, then there is no one there to create new things, and therefore nothing new can begin.

This is why Paul, one of the wisest men ever to live, wrote the following words:

What can be known about God is plain to them, because God has shown it to them. **For God's invisible attributes**, namely, **his eternal power** and divine nature, **have been clearly perceived, ever since the creation of the world, in the things that have been made.** So they are without excuse. (Romans 1:19–20 ESV)

God's eternal power — the fact that He always exists, an eternal Being with no beginning — is clearly perceived in all things that have beginnings.

Without a Being who always exists, there is no one there to begin new things.

Question 4

When will the star of Bethlehem be visible again?[9]

Tonight, you look into the sky and see the Star yourself.

That might sound ridiculous at first. If the Star of Bethlehem was visible today, wouldn't we notice?

The answer is that we notice the Star today just as most people in the ancient world did. Which is to say, we see it, but we don't recognize its significance.

Let me cut to heart of it: **the Star of Bethlehem is Jupiter.**

Again, that sounds ridiculous. Jupiter is a planet, not a star. Further, how could Jupiter lead the way for the Magi, or come to rest over Bethlehem?

First, the word Matthew uses in Greek, *astera*, can refer to a traditional star, but also a planet (a moving "star"), or a comet or meteor. Thus Jupiter is a contender for the position of the Star.

Second, **using modern computer technology, we can turn the night sky back to the time of Jesus and watch Jupiter perform every action that Matthew's Gospel describes the Star doing.**

And it's simply stunning.

To find the Star, let's start in Matthew's Gospel and take note of everything we can learn about this elusive nighttime guide:

> Now after Jesus was born in Bethlehem of Judea in the days of Herod the king, behold, wise men from the east came to Jerusalem, saying, "Where is he who has been **born king** of the **Jews**? For **we saw his star in the east** and have come to **worship** him." (Matthew 2:1–2 ESV)

The details appear fast and quick. From these two verses, we glean five details:

1. Something about the Star signified *kingship*

2. Something about the Star pointed to the King being from the *Jewish people*

3. Something about the Star pointed to the King being *born*

4. The star rose *in the east*, like most other stars

5. They were prepared to *worship* the person this Star celebrated

This is a good start, but we need more:

> When Herod the king heard this, he was troubled, and all Jerusalem with him [...] Then Herod summoned the wise men secretly and ascertained from them **what time the star had appeared.** (Matthew 2:3, 7 ESV)

This one takes a bit more detective work, but we can still glean two important details:

6. The Star appeared *at an exact time*

7. Herod and all those in Jerusalem *had missed it completely*

These details are vital. First, they tell us that the Star was a real event in the skies that happened at a precise time. Second, they tell us that it was an easy event to miss, if you weren't paying attention.

A lot of movies depict the Star as a giant glowing object (typically shaped like a cross) with a ray of light pointing straight to Jesus' manger. That never happened. Such a sign would be impossible to miss at night in a society with little-to-no nighttime illumination.

(It wasn't like this.)

We only need a few more points, now:

> And he sent them to Bethlehem, saying, "Go and search diligently for the child, and when you have found him, bring me word, that I too may come and worship him." After listening to the king, they went on their way. And behold, **the star that they had seen when it rose went before them until it came to rest over the place where the child was**. When they saw the star, they rejoiced exceedingly with great joy. (Matthew 2:8–10 ESV)

8. The Star *endured over a long period of time*. They had seen it in the East and traveled to Israel, yet the Star was still visible to them from Jerusalem.

9. The Star *went ahead of them* on the journey from Jerusalem to Bethlehem.

10. The Star *stopped* in the sky.

We have our ten data points. Now let's compare them to Jupiter as it dances its way across the ancient skies.

For our first three points, we need something that establishes **kingship,** *birth,* *and the* **Jewish** **people.** Does Jupiter give us that? Indeed it does:

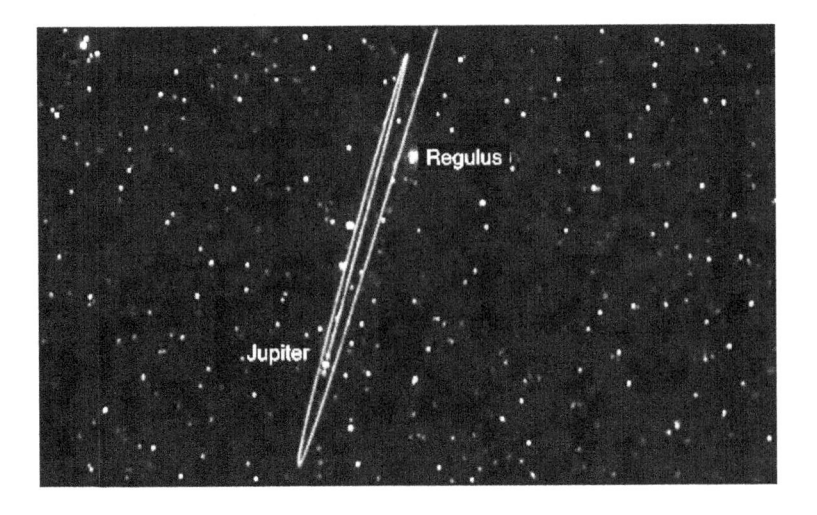

In this picture[10], you're witnessing a coronation of kings.

Jupiter, the largest planet in the solar system, was always associated with royalty, even from ancient times. It was unambiguously the King Planet.

By the same token, Regulus was the King Star. It was brighter than nearly anything else in the nighttime sky. (If you haven't heard of Regulus lately, don't be surprised. Today, we can zoom in and discern that Regulus is actually *four* stars which exist so closely together that they appeared to be a singular entity to those without telescopes. This is why is shone so brightly and was thus recognized as the King Star).

Jupiter passes Regulus once every 12 years or so. Typically, they go on their merry ways.

But in 3 B.C. they do something spectacular.

Jupiter passes Regulus, as always. Then it loops back around and passes Regulus again. Then it loops back around a third time and completes a third pass by Regulus — in effect, drawing a crown. **In September of 3 B.C., the King Planet crowns the King Star.**

This triple conjunction is *exceedingly* rare. Yet it's also exceedingly easy to miss, if you're not paying attention. Anyone randomly looking up at the night sky would see nothing different; there was no supernova burst or comet streaking by. But if you were an astronomer studying the sky night after night, it would knock your socks off. You would never have seen anything like it.

So we have our first qualification: the King Planet crowning the King Star certainly signifies kingship.

But what of the connection to the Jewish people?

23

For this, we turn to Genesis, and look at the particular description given to Judah, forever to be associated with his descendants:

> **Judah is a lion's cub**; from the prey, my son, you have gone up. He stooped down; he crouched as a lion and as a lioness; who dares rouse him? **The scepter shall not depart from Judah, nor the ruler's staff from between his feet**, until tribute comes to him; and to him shall be the obedience of the peoples. (Genesis 49:9–10 ESV)

From the beginning of Israel's existence as a clan, **the lion signified the tribe of Judah**. This symbolism carried over as Israel's identity became uniquely Jewish. The symbol has been carried into the modern day, as the emblem of Jerusalem features the Lion of Judah front-and-center.

Is a lion present in Jupiter's coronation of Regulus?

Yes, in fact.

The entire coronation happened within the constellation of Leo, the Lion. It also began precisely on the Jewish New Year.

So we have *kingship* and we have *Jewish people*. But what about the Star signifies *birth*? If this conjunction signified a conception of a new king, we should expect something to happen nine months later.

And indeed, nine months later Jupiter the King Planet is "birthed" out of Venus, the Mother Planet.

In June of 2 BC Jupiter approaches Venus. Both planets were shining at their brightest. When they neared, they did not cover each other, but rather aligned immediately next to each other. In so doing, they added their brilliance together and became the brightest star in the sky.

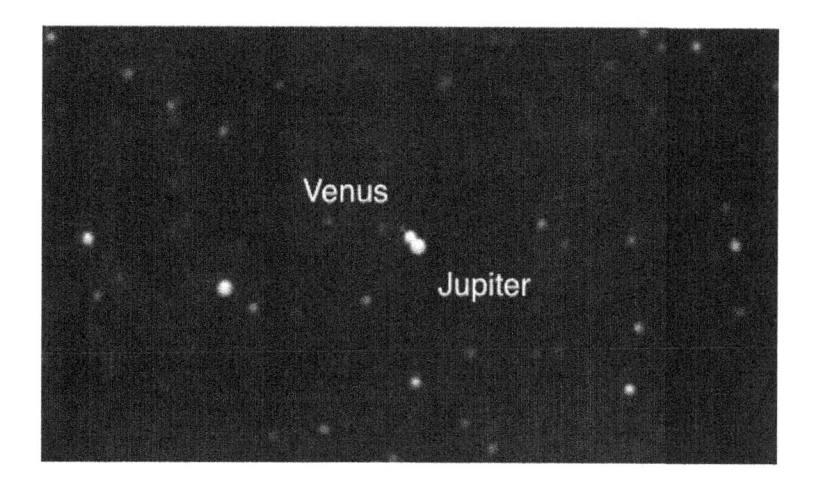

Today, you can see this conjunction replayed in many planetariums around Christmastime. It makes for a spectacular show.

So we have **kingship**, the **Jewish people**, and **birth**. The coronation signifies conception, and nine months later the King Planet emerges from the Mother Planet in the brightest display in the nighttime sky.

We also have four further qualifications met: the Star rose *in the east*, just as most stars do. It appeared *at a precise time*, such that anyone making note of the paths of the planets could reproduce it from their observations. Also, it was visible, but it was **missed completely** by Herod

25

and everyone in Jerusalem. To anyone not paying attention, the planets were simply moving as they always do. But to astronomers who studied the skies, the symbology arrested their attention. Finally, the Star *endured over time*, such that the Magi could witness the coronation and birth in the sky, then travel to Jerusalem to seek out this newborn king.

But now we have a seemingly impossible task: the Star must *go ahead of the Magi to Bethlehem* and *stop in the sky* above the place where Jesus was born.

Did Jupiter ever do such a thing?

Yes, it actually does both.

After the Magi witnessed the conjunction of Jupiter and Venus in June of 2 BC, they began traveling. Such a journey would take a few months, particularly if they were coming from the regions around Babylon, where a great many people of Jewish descent still lived at the time.

It's entirely reasonable to suppose that they arrived in Jerusalem at December of 2 BC. If they did, and they looked south to Bethlehem (which lay a mere five miles away), they would witness Jupiter standing directly above Bethlehem in the night sky.

Jupiter pointed the way directly from Jerusalem to Bethlehem.

But to fulfill what Matthew describes, Jupiter needs to *stop* in the sky. Can it do that?

Indeed it can, and indeed it did.

As the Magi watched, Jupiter entered retrograde motion. In other words, it was traveling in one direction across the sky, then it stopped, and went back the way it came.

On precisely December 25th of 2 BC, Jupiter came to a full stop in the sky immediately over Bethlehem.

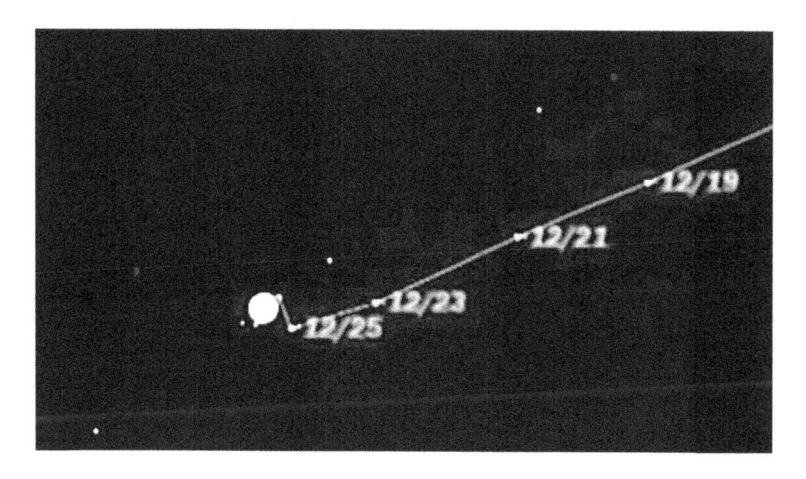

In so doing, Jupiter fulfills all of the qualifications that Matthew describes.

All except one: *worship.* The Magi came not merely to pay homage to this newborn King, but to worship Him.

Whoever these Magi were, it is clear that they knew the Hebrew Scriptures. They knew to associate the Lion with the tribe of Judah. They knew a King, Messiah the Prince, was prophesied to be born precisely around this time. They knew that this King would be no mere human, but that this King, even as a helpless baby, deserved their worship.

27

Who did they understand this King to be?

700 years before the Star began singing in the night sky, Isaiah the prophet told us precisely who this King would be:

> For to us **a child is born**, to us a son is given; and the government shall be upon his shoulder, and his name shall be called Wonderful Counselor, **Mighty God**, **Everlasting Father**, Prince of Peace. (Isaiah 9:6 ESV)

The Magi came to worship this King, believing that He was Mighty God, the Everlasting Father, born as a child in the flesh.

This is how they found the baby Jesus.

Question 5

The shepherd is a prominent, meaningful metaphor in the Bible. But why do the prophets ask us to think of Messiah as our Good Shepherd?[11]

The Hebrew people always think **visually**.

The phrase "God will keep you safe" is weak. *How* will God keep me safe? What should I expect that to look like? Will He keep me safe like a jailor keeps a prisoner safe, or like a merchant keeps his coins safe, or like a general keeps his troops safe? What is God's heart toward me as He keeps me safe?

There's no way to tell, from such a weak phrase.

Compare that to the rich, visual, personal way Jesus describes Himself:

> **"I am the good shepherd**. The good shepherd lays down his life for the sheep. He who is a hired hand and not a shepherd, who does not own the sheep, sees the wolf coming and leaves the sheep and flees, and the wolf snatches them and scatters them. He flees because he is a hired hand and cares nothing

for the sheep. **I am the good shepherd.** I know my own and my own know me, just as the Father knows me and I know the Father; and I lay down my life for the sheep. And I have other sheep that are not of this fold. I must bring them also, and they will listen to my voice. So there will be one flock, one shepherd." (John 10:11-16 ESV)

Jesus unveils His heart clearly. He cares for His people so much that He willingly lays down His life to keep them safe. He cannot be bribed or chased away through fear like a hired hand. No one can stop Jesus from caring for those He loves.

The Bible describes this image of a Good Shepherd so often because it communicates so much. The original audience immediately grasped its meaning. It communicates God's love and devotion to His people as well as His actions on their behalf.

Finally, the Bible calls Jesus the Good Shepherd to distinguish Him from the bad shepherds who held power in Israel at the time. Many spiritual leaders were like the hired servant: they cared more for themselves than their people.

Some took this selfishness to the extreme: they stole money and property from widows, used their prominence in the community for personal gain, lorded their position over others, or excluded other races from their gatherings.

Bad shepherds are in it for themselves.

But Jesus, the Good Shepherd, is in this for the sheep. He will lay down His life to keep them safe, because He cares for them.

That's the way He loves you.

Question 6

What is the hardest thing to believe in the Bible?[12]

That God loves me.

That God created me, knows everything about me, measured every success and failure I'll ever commit, memorized all my thoughts before I was even born… and yet He still loves me.

I know it's true. I rejoice that it's true.

But it's still the hardest thing I have ever believed.

Question 7

Is it true that many Christians believe that both heaven and hell are a state of mind rather than an actual place?[13]

Yes, a few Christians believe this. They are a tiny minority, but they certainly exist.

These Christians are generally uncomfortable with the idea of heaven and hell as literal places. They re-define them as states of mind to make the concepts feel more palatable.

The problem with this approach is that you have to throw away most of what Jesus said about heaven and hell.

One other answer to this question posits that we have no facts about heaven and hell, only rumors. But Jesus provides us with facts. We don't want guesses about what heaven and hell are like; we want the facts from the only Person who could possibly tell us: God Himself.

Jesus speaks about hell and heaven frequently. His warnings and invitations are sharp and clear. One example is the following:

> You serpents, you brood of vipers, how are you to escape being sentenced to hell? Therefore I send you prophets and wise men and scribes, some of whom you will kill and crucify, and some you will flog in your synagogues and persecute from town to town. (Matthew 23:33-34, ESV)

Jesus consistently describes hell and heaven as literal places. In the quote above, it is a place you can be sentenced to. If He had meant a frame of mind instead, there would be no point in talking about sentencing, because the Pharisees He was addressing were already locked into a frame of mind that rejected God and sought to kill those they disagreed with.

To circle back to the question: Yes, a few Christians believe hell and heaven to be states of mind. But they believe this contrary to what Jesus taught.

The vast majority of Christians, today and throughout history, accept heaven and hell as literal places, because that's how Christ depicts them.

Question 8

Why and how should I read the Bible?[14]

Let's take these in pieces.

Why should I read the Bible?

Because it will improve your life in nearly every major area.

How should I read the Bible?

As though your life depended on it.

Researchers at the Center of Bible Engagement recently discovered that **when a person reads the Bible at least four times a week**, it affects nearly every major area of their lives in positive ways:

6. Feelings of loneliness dropped 30%

7. Anger issues dropped 32%

8. Bitterness in relationships (marriage, children, relatives) dropped 40%

9. Alcoholism dropped 57%

10. Feeling spiritually stagnant dropped 60%

11. Viewing pornography dropped 62%

12. Gambling dropped 64%

13. Sharing the Gospel increased 200%

14. Discipling others increased 230%[15]

Interestingly, these results didn't appear until people read the Bible **four times each week**. For those who read the Bible once, twice, or three times a week, their statistics in each of these areas were virtually identical to people who don't read the Bible at all.

But as soon as you bump up to four times a week, the results skyrocket. Those who read the Bible daily had the best results of all.

Some may suspect these results of being biased. After all, don't the researchers want you to read the Bible more?

But the researchers lay out everything in the paper above. The results persisted, even when controlling for age, church attendance, prayer, and so on. The single most predictive factor on whether you'll experience the benefits above is how often you read the Bible. **Opening the Word at least four times weekly unlocks a whole slew of benefits that simply don't appear for those who read it less.**

Jesus really meant what He said when He declared, *"I have come to give you life, and life abundantly!"* (John 10:10)

So let me ask:

Do you want to feel less lonely?

Do you want to feel more peaceful and be able to control your anger?

Do you want healthier relationships?

Do you want to reduce alcohol's hold on you?

Do you want to feel spiritually vibrant?

Do you want to stop losing money and time to porn and gambling?

Doesn't everybody want these things?

The key to receiving them is so simple: read your Bible at least four times a week.

If you're skeptical, you can experiment easily. Read the Bible daily for a month. Read it as you read good books: read it to learn, read it to discover beauty, read it for wisdom, read it for entertainment, read it for guidance, read it for hope. Read it to draw near to God.

After a month of this, compare how you feel in each of these areas to how you felt before you started.

If the science above is accurate, it will be worth your time.

Question 9

Can anyone explain the Trinity in simple language? I have been struggling with it for over 20 years and no priest was able to give a convincing explanation.[16]

For this answer, let's turn to logic and mathematics — two essential tools for spiritual conversations.

Logic

You can teach the logic of the Holy Trinity with seven simple propositions, all of which are supported by the Bible.

1. God is one God. (Deut. 6:4, NET: *"The LORD our God, the LORD is one!"*)

2. The Father is God. (Matt. 6:9, NET: *"Our Father in Heaven..."*)

3. Jesus, the Son, is God. (Col 2:9, NET: *"For in Christ all the fullness of the Deity lives in bodily form..."*)

4. The Holy Spirit is God. (Acts 5:3–4, NET: *"...why has Satan filled your heart to lie to the Holy Spirit? [...] You have not lied to man but to God!"*)

5. The Father is not the Son. (John 16:28, NET: *"I [Jesus] came from the Father..."*)

6. The Son is not the Spirit. (John 14:16–17, NET: *"I [Jesus] will ask the Father, and He will give you another Advocate to be with you forever — the Spirit of Truth."*)

7. The Spirit is not the Father. (John 15:26, NET: *"...the Spirit of Truth who goes out from the Father..."*)

These seven propositions are all that you need to formulate a comprehensive description of the Holy Trinity.

Mathematics

Describing the Trinity is simple with math — providing that you use the right kind of math.

Adding 1+1+1 will only get you 3. But this is not the correct kind of math to use. The number 1 is finite. But God has always revealed Himself as infinite.

What happens when you add together three infinities? You end up with infinity.

So describing the Trinity in mathematics is as simple as this:

Infinity + Infinity + Infinity = Infinity

So far so good. But let's take this a bit further.

How would you define the Trinity in non-biblical terms?

The math used above would be a good example. In mathematics, we can study the concept of infinity. We have a good idea of how it works. We can use it profitably in a wide variety of equations.

It demonstrates how real and practical it is to have a limitless subject. A limitless number exists and we know how it works. Starting from this, we can much more easily approach the idea of a limitless Person who exists and understand a bit more clearly how He works.

Is there proof the Trinity exists?

Yes. This is why the Bible was written — because people had witnessed this truth and wanted to spread this truth to others.

Some will object and say that the Bible can't be used as proof of the Trinity. To this I ask: why not? The entire purpose of the Bible was to record the proof of God acting in history and to spread this truth around the world. Why would you discount as proof the very document whose entire purpose is to be the proof that the Trinity exists?

To proceed, then: the Trinity is present throughout the entire Bible, both in the Old and New Testaments.

Many will object, saying that the word "Trinity" is never mentioned. The term "Trinity" was indeed coined later, in order to provide a short-hand word to refer to what the Bible says about God. But **the theology of God being one God, yet having three Persons, is present constantly throughout the Bible.**

One of the clearest pictures happens at the start of Jesus' public ministry. It is mentioned in all four Gospels, but I'll give you Matthew's perspective for now:

> Then Jesus came from Galilee to John to be baptized by him in the Jordan River. But John tried to prevent him, saying, "I need to be baptized by you, and yet you come to me?" So Jesus replied to him, "Let it happen now, for it is right for us to fulfill all righteousness." Then John yielded to him. After Jesus was baptized, just as **he was coming up out of the water**, the heavens opened and he saw the **Spirit of God descending like a dove** and coming on him. And **a voice from heaven said**, "This is my one dear Son; in him I take great delight." (Matthew 3:13–17 NET)

We see here God presented in all three Persons, clearly and unambiguously:

- God the Father speaks aloud from Heaven, saying *"This is my one dear Son; in him I take great delight."*

- God the Son, Jesus, stands on the riverbank.

- God the Spirit descends on Jesus like a dove.

God the Father is not the Son. God the Son is not the Spirit. God the Spirit is not the Father. They are each located in different places in this moment.

Yet at the same time, we have verses like Deuteronomy 6:4, which is called the *shema*: "Hear, O Israel: the LORD our God, the LORD is one!"

Thus, whatever else God is, He must be one God. He is not three Gods. Despite having three Persons, He is solely and exclusively one God.

Early Christians needed a phrase to refer to this whole jumble of facts. They ended up creating the term "Trinity" to express the tri-fold unity of God.

The term "Trinity" was not coined until a few hundred years after the New Testament was completed. Some people confuse this with the idea of the Trinity being invented hundreds of years later.

But the concepts that the Trinity refers to have been in the Bible from the beginning. It clearly presents God as one God, yet having three Persons: the Father, the Son, and the Spirit.

Question 10

How do I grow my faith in Christianity?
I'm still young and have big dreams and aspirations, but want to achieve them the right way, in God's word. I have good days and praise him a lot but when the days going bad, I start to doubt him. How do I change?[17]

First, let me say how much I appreciate this question! It is so honest, and yet the heart behind it is so sincere.

I'm going to focus on the first part of this question: *"How do I grow my faith?"* As we address that, it will naturally answer the rest of the questions.

On the surface, we often think the problem is not having enough faith. But having a small amount of faith is never the problem.

At one point, Jesus' disciples pleaded with Him, *"Increase our faith!"*

How did Jesus respond? If being low on faith was the problem, then Jesus would have told them how to get more faith, so they could fix their problem.

But Jesus said the opposite:

> "If you had *faith like a grain of mustard seed*, you could say to this mulberry tree, 'Be uprooted and planted in the sea,' and it would obey you.'" (Luke 17:5–6, ESV)

A mustard seed was one of the smallest items the disciples could understand, so small it's nearly invisible when placed in the middle of your hand.

A faith that small — so small it's nearly invisible — can still accomplish miracles.

Jewish teachers commonly used exaggerated word pictures to drive a point home. Jesus' image of a mulberry tree jumping out of the ground and rushing into the sea illustrated His point: if you have even the smallest amount of faith, you can still accomplish more than you could ever imagine.

Why? Shouldn't the disciples need a massive amount of faith to move a tree?

No. **Faith is not like money.** You can't purchase bigger and bigger answers by having more and more faith.

Faith is trust.

Do you trust God? If so, then you'll trust Him with your requests. Trust doesn't mean that you force God to answer in the way you prefer. It means you trust Him to handle the situation in the way that He knows best.

Many times, when I talk with people who feel low on faith, the real situation is this: they trusted God with a request — and God didn't handle it the way they wanted.

This is what shatters faith in so many. They thought faith was like money, and they thought they could buy the answer they wanted from God with enough faith. But God didn't do what they wanted. So their faith in Him diminished.

But this is the key: that wasn't faith at all.

Again, **faith is trust**. If you trust God with your request, then you trust that He will answer it in the best possible way — even if it's the opposite of what you wanted.

Jesus showed us what this kind of faith looks like in the Garden of Gethsemane. When Jesus prayed in Gethsemane, He knew that the Father's plan was for Jesus to be nailed to a Cross and killed the next morning. Jesus pleaded in prayer: "Father, if You are willing, please take this cup of suffering away from me. *Yet I want Your will to be done, not mine"* (Luke 22:42 NLT).

Jesus trusted the Father with His request. He prayed specifically: let me avoid this suffering if there is any possible way.

Yet Jesus did not view faith as money. He didn't try to buy the specific answer that He wanted with enough faith. Instead, Jesus trusted the Father with the decision: *"Yet I want Your will to be done, not mine."*

This is real faith!

If you trust God with your requests, you will see Him amaze you constantly.

To be clear: the answer might not always be what you want. Jesus certainly didn't want to suffer on the Cross! But the answer was still *good*. By suffering on the Cross, Jesus purchased eternal life for all who choose to follow Him. We could never have been saved otherwise.

So if faith is trust, how do we build more faith? How do we learn to trust God more?

The answers are simple — but incredibly powerful:

- **Keep track of God's faithfulness to you.** Pray daily and ask God to handle all the scenarios you find yourself in. Keep track of everything you ask. Then — and this is the fun part — keep track of how God handles each one. Write down how He answers each prayer, even if it's not the way that you envisioned at first. As you build a visible record of God's faithfulness in your daily requests, you'll learn to trust Him more and more.

- If you want to know how to pray, or what to pray for, read the Bible. Pay attention to the way people pray and how God answers their prayers. **Study how God answers prayer.** It will teach you how to pray for the people in your life, and it will teach you how to spot God's answers.

- **Talk to other Christians about how God has been faithful to them.** Let other Christians encourage your faith by telling you about the God who is faithful. These can be Christians in your life or Christians whose stories are recorded in biographies. If you'd like a recommendation, start with George Mueller or Billy Graham.

- Finally — and perhaps most powerfully — **take the leap to obey God in the places you're afraid to.** When we obey God, faith explodes, because we see that God truly is faithful to keep His promises. Consider forgiveness: when people finally forgive after a lifetime of hatred, they experience God's faithfulness as He floods their souls with peace. Consider confession: when people confess their sins to God, they experience God's faithfulness as God forgives them, and for the first time they feel clean. Consider giving: when people give the resources they have to help others, they experience God's faithfulness as He provides back for them. Consider joy: when people seek God with all their hearts, they experience God's faithfulness, because they find Him. And in Him, they find their heart's true delight.

Ultimately, if you do nothing, your faith will die — just as a romantic relationship will die if you never do anything with the other person.

But if you choose to trust God to handle your requests and you choose to obey what He's calling you to do, your faith will skyrocket.

I promise you: as your trust in God grows, He will guide you faithfully in your life. He will never leave you, and never forsake you (Hebrews 13:5).

Question 11

Unlike other failed Messiahs, why did Jesus' message endure after his death?[18]

Because Jesus didn't fail as Messiah.

He accomplished everything the Law and the Prophets said Messiah would do — in His first advent.

Up until the prophet Daniel wrote, everyone expected Messiah to come once, and usher in the Kingdom of God forever. But in Daniel's prophecy, God specified that Messiah would come once and be cut off for His people. More than that, Jerusalem itself would be destroyed.

Before Daniel, no one expected Messiah to die. After Daniel, it was unavoidable that Messiah would have to die.

Or to say it differently: **for Messiah to be successful, He had to die. Daniel leaves no other option.**

Let's walk through this. I'll break the verse down into individual sections to help us grasp all it contains:

> Seventy weeks[?] have been determined concerning your people and your holy city
> to put an end to[?] rebellion,

> to bring sin⸆ to completion,⸆
> to atone for iniquity,
> to bring in perpetual⸆ righteousness,
> to seal up⸆ the prophetic vision,⸆
> and to anoint a most holy place.⸆
> (Daniel 9:24 NET)

This is Messiah's mission. All of these things happen when Messiah ushers in the Kingdom of God forever.

Daniel desired for us to know who Messiah is and what He needed to accomplish. The verse above tells us what Messiah will do. But we need certainty to know who this Messiah will be.

Through prophecy, Daniel provides this, as well. He gives us a precise clock from which to calculate the exact day of Messiah's appearing:

> So know and understand: **From the issuing of the command⸆ to restore and rebuild Jerusalem⸆ until Messiah the Prince arrives**,⸆ there will be a period of seven weeks⸆ and sixty-two weeks. It will again be built,⸆ with plaza and moat, but in distressful times. (Daniel 9:25 NET)

Artaxerxes issued the decree to rebuild the walls of Jerusalem on March 5 444 B.C. The "week" is a group of seven years. Seven weeks plus sixty-two weeks yields sixty-nine weeks, or 483 years.

51

The Jewish calendar uses 360 days per year, being a lunar calendar. 483 years of 360 days takes you straight to March 29, 33 A.D. – *the very Sunday that Jesus entered Jerusalem in the Triumphal Entry.*

Thus, we know with certainty this prophecy refers to Jesus as Messiah.

Now that Messiah's identity is certified, Daniel gives us the most shocking piece of Messiah's mission:

> **Now after the sixty-two weeks, Messiah will be cut off and have nothing.** As for the city and the sanctuary, the people of the coming prince will destroy⃞ them. (Daniel 9:26 NET)

Immediately after the seven weeks and sixty-two weeks finish, Messiah will be cut off.

And indeed, five days after arriving in Jerusalem, Jesus was cut off. He was killed on April 3, 33 A.D.

Jesus fulfilled this Messianic prophecy to the letter.

But this isn't the of the story.

The first verse above states Messiah's mission: to put an end to⃞ rebellion, to bring sin⃞ to completion,⃞ to atone for iniquity, to bring in perpetual⃞ righteousness, to seal up⃞ the prophetic vision,⃞ and to anoint a most holy place.⃞

Most of these are yet to be fulfilled. Jesus atoned first iniquity on the Cross as He died, but righteousness is not yet perpetual, and rebellion has not yet ended.

Messiah's death was necessary to atone for iniquity. As Leviticus 17:11 states, there is no forgiveness of sin without the shedding of blood:

> "For the life of the flesh is in the blood, and I have given it for you on the altar to make atonement for your souls, for **it is the blood that makes atonement by the life**."

Messiah needed to atone for iniquity. For that, He had to die.

Messiah also needs to usher in the Kingdom of God, completing the rest of the mission above. For that, He needs to live again.

Three days after dying on the Cross, Jesus rose again.

But then we have another problem: Jerusalem must be destroyed, yet Messiah must inaugurate the eternal Kingdom of God.

The answer is that Messiah, over whom death no longer has any hold, will come again.

40 days after Jesus rose from death, He ascended to the Father. Jesus could not inaugurate the Kingdom yet. Daniel's prophecy was not complete: Jerusalem had to fall.

Nearly 40 years after Jesus ascended, Rome destroyed Jerusalem and its Temple. Daniel's prophecy was complete: as for the city and the sanctuary, the people of the coming prince had destroyed them.

But this is not the end for Jerusalem.

The people of God would return to the land of Israel and to Jerusalem. They did In 1947 and 1967.

They had to.

Messiah will return to His people. He must, to put an end to rebellion, to establish righteousness forever — and "**to anoint a most holy place.**"

Could this holy place be anywhere else but Jerusalem?

Jesus is the only One who could possibly fulfill Daniel 9:24–26. He fulfilled it to the letter.

Question 12

Do you find it incomprehensible that despite the track record of science in improving people's lives, evangelicals will still give greater credence to blind acceptance of Scripture?[19]

These two things aren't at odds.

I'm an Evangelical Christian. **I love science *because* I love the Scriptures.**

There is no strife between the Bible and science. They harmonize beautifully.

How so? **Because the Scriptures command us to explore the universe scientifically. It's something God *wants* us to do:**

- God designed nature to be studied: *"It is the glory of God to conceal things, but the glory of kings is to search things out."* (Proverbs 25:2 ESV)

- Solomon, one of the best kings of Israel, loved the scientific study of nature: *"He produced manuals on botany, describing every kind of plant, from the cedars of Lebanon to the hyssop that grows on* walls. He also produced manuals on biology, describing animals, birds, insects, and fish." (1 Kings 4:33 NET)

- The Scriptures describe the study of nature as the revelation of God's glory: *"The heavens proclaim the glory of God; the skies display his craftsmanship. Day after day they continue to speak; night after night they make him known. They speak without a sound or word; their voice is never heard. Yet their message has gone throughout the earth, and their words to all the world."* (Psalm 19:1–4 NLT)

Those who love the Scriptures need fear no truth. If indeed God created the universe, then all truth belongs to Him. There are no scientific truths to fear. There's no reason for anyone who loves the Bible to resist science!

As you study history, you'll find that **many of the most influential scientists are devout Christians.**

The website famousscientists.org put together an incredible list of God-fearing scientists (so many more could be added!) who have made vast contributions to the advancement of science:

Robert Boyle, 1627 – 1691. Said that a deeper understanding of science was a higher glorification of God. Defined elements, compounds, and mixtures. Discovered the first gas law – Boyle's Law.

Antoine Lavoisier, 1743 – 1794. A Roman Catholic believer in the authenticity of the Holy Scriptures. A founder of modern chemistry; discovered oxygen's role in combustion and respiration; discovered that water is a compound of hydrogen and oxygen;

Leonhard Euler, 1707 – 1783. The son of a Calvinist pastor. Wrote religious texts and is commemorated by the Lutheran Church on their Calendar of Saints. Published more mathematics than any other single mathematician in history, much of it brilliant and groundbreaking.

Michael Faraday, 1791 – 1867. A devout member and elder of the Sandemanian Church. Discovered electromagnetic induction; discovered the first experimental link between light and magnetism; carried out the first room-temperature liquefaction of a gas.

James Clerk Maxwell, 1831 – 1879. An evangelical Protestant who learned the Bible by heart at age 14. Transformed our understanding of nature: his famous equations unified the forces of electricity and magnetism, indicating that light is an electromagnetic wave. His kinetic theory established that temperature is entirely dependent on the speeds of particles.

Gregor Mendel, 1822 – 1884. A Roman Catholic Augustinian abbot. Founded the science of genetics; identified many of the mathematical rules of heredity; identified recessive and dominant traits.

Arthur Compton, 1892 – 1962. A deacon in the Baptist Church. Discovered that light can behave as a particle as well as a wave, and coined the word photon to describe a particle of light.

Ronald Fisher, 1890 – 1962. A devout Anglican: made religious broadcasts, and wrote religious articles. Unified evolution by natural selection with

Mendel's rules of inheritance, so defining the new field of population genetics. Invented experimental design; devised the statistical concept of variance.

Bernhard Riemann, 1826 – 1866. Son of a Lutheran pastor. A devout Christian who died reciting the Lord's Prayer. Transformed geometry providing the foundation of Einstein's theory of general relativity; the Riemann hypothesis has become the most famous unresolved problem in mathematics.

Georges Lemaître, 1894 – 1966. Roman Catholic priest. Discovered that space and the universe are expanding; discovered Hubble's law; proposed the universe began with the explosion of a 'primeval atom' whose matter spread and evolved to form the galaxies and stars we observe today.

Isaac Newton, 1643 to 1727. Passionate dissenting Protestant who spent more time on Bible study than math and physics. Profoundly changed our understanding of nature with his law of universal gravitation and his laws of motion; invented calculus; built the first ever reflecting telescope; showed sunlight is made of all the colors of the rainbow.

Charles Townes, 1915 – 2015. A member of the United Church of Christ. Prayed daily. Wrote books linking science and religion; believed religion more important than science. Invented the laser and maser. Established that the Milky Way has a supermassive black hole at its center.

Mary Anning, 1799 – 1847. A devoted Anglican, spent her spare time reading the Bible. Discovered the first complete specimen of a plesiosaur; deduced the diets of dinosaurs.

Willard Gibbs, 1839 – 1903. Member of the Congregational Church who attended services every week. Invented vector analysis and founded the sciences of modern statistical mechanics and chemical thermodynamics.

John Dalton, 1766 – 1844. A faithful Quaker who lived modestly. Dalton's Atomic Theory is the basis of chemistry; discovered Gay-Lussac's Law relating temperature, volume, and pressure of gases; discovered the law of partial gas pressures.

Carl Friedrich Gauss, 1777 – 1855. A Lutheran Protestant who believed science revealed the immortal human soul and that there is complete unity between science and God. Gauss revolutionized number theory and invented the method of least squares and the fast Fourier transform. His profound contributions to the physical sciences include Gauss's Law & Gauss's Law for Magnetism.

Charles Barkla, 1877 – 1944. A Methodist who believed science was part of his quest for God. Discovered that atoms have the same number of electrons as their atomic number and that X-rays emitted by excited atoms are 'fingerprints' for the atom.

George Washington Carver, 1864 – 1943. A Protestant Evangelist and Bible class leader whose faith in Jesus was the mechanism through which he carried out his scientific work. Improved the agricultural economy of the USA by promoting nitrogen providing peanuts as an alternative crop to cotton to prevent soil depletion.

Francis Collins 1950 – present. Atheist turned devout Christian. Invented positional cloning. Took part in discovery of the genes for cystic fibrosis, Huntington's disease, and neurofibromatosis. Directed National Human Genome Research Institute for 15 years.

Ernest Walton, 1903 – 1995. A devout Methodist, who said science was a way of knowing more about God. Winner of the Nobel Prize in Physics after he artificially split the atom and proved that E = mc2.

Florence Nightingale, 1820 – 1910. An Anglican who believed God spoke to her, calling her to her work. Transformed nursing into a respected, highly trained profession; used statistics to analyze wider health outcomes; advocated sanitary reforms largely credited with adding 20 years to life expectancy between 1871 and 1935.

J. J. Thomson, 1856 – 1940. A practicing Anglican who prayed and read the Bible daily. Discovered the electron; invented one of the most powerful tools in analytical chemistry – the mass spectrometer; obtained the first evidence for isotopes of stable elements.

Alessandro Volta, 1745 – 1827. A Roman Catholic who declared that he had never wavered in his faith. Invented the electric battery; wrote the first electromotive series; isolated methane for the first time.

Blaise Pascal, 1623 – 1662. A Roman Catholic theologian. Pascal's wager justifies belief in God. Devised Pascal's triangle for the binomial coefficients and co-founded probability theory. Invented the hydraulic press and the mechanical calculator.

William Thomson (Lord Kelvin), 1824 – 1907. An elder of the Free Church of Scotland. Codified the first two laws of thermodynamics, deduced the absolute zero of temperature is -273.15 °C. On the Kelvin scale, absolute zero is found at 0 kelvin. Invented the signalling equipment used in the first transatlantic telegraph via an undersea cable.

Charles Babbage, 1791 – 1871. A Protestant devotee who devoted a chapter of his autobiography to a discussion of his faith. The father of the computer, invented the Analytical Engine, a Turing Complete computer in 1837 – the first general purpose computer.

Werner Heisenberg, 1901 – 1976. A Lutheran with deep Christian convictions. One of the primary creators of quantum mechanics. Formulated the Heisenberg Uncertainty Principle.

Albrecht von Haller, 1708 – 1777. A Protestant, wrote religious texts and helped organize the construction of the Reformed Church in Göttingen. The father of modern physiology.

Nicolas Steno, 1638 – 1686. Born a Lutheran, converted to Catholicism and became a bishop. Beatified in 1988, the third of four steps needed to be declared a saint. One of the founders of modern geology and stratigraphy.

Humphry Davy, 1778 – 1829. Said that God's design was revealed by chemical investigations. Discovered the electrical nature of chemical bonding. Used electricity to split several substances into their basic building blocks for the first time, discovering chlorine and iodine; produced the first ever samples of the elements barium, boron, calcium, magnesium, potassium, sodium, and strontium. Invented the safety lamp.

Arthur Eddington, 1882 – 1944. A Quaker, who believed the hand that made us is Divine. He was the first scientist to propose stars obtain their energy from nuclear fusion. Experimentally verified Einstein's General Theory of Relativity.

John Ambrose Fleming, 1849 – 1945. A devout Christian who preached about the Resurrection and founded the creationist Evolution Protest Movement. Founded the electronic age with his invention of the vacuum tube (thermionic valve); devised the hand rules for electric motors and generators.

Samuel Morse, 1791 – 1872. A Calvinist with Unitarian sympathies who funded a lectureship considering the relation of the Bible to the Sciences. Took part in the invention of a single-wire telegraph and patented it. Developed the Morse code.

John Eccles, 1903 – 1997. Christian and sometimes practicing Roman Catholic. Believed in a Divine Providence operating over and above the materialistic happenings of biological evolution. Winner of the Nobel Prize in Physiology or Medicine for his work on the physiology of synapses.[20]

"34 Great Scientists Who Were Committed Christians," accessed at https://www.famousscientists.org/great-scientists-christians/

Do I thus find it incomprehensible that despite the track record of science in improving people's lives, evangelicals will still give greater credence to blind acceptance of scripture?

Far from it.

Evangelicals will continue to follow the Scriptures, because it is the Scriptures themselves that propel us to pursue the advancement of science.

Question 13

What parts of the New Testament have been significantly edited?[21]

None.

The oldest manuscripts are virtually identical to what you'd pick up in a bookstore today.

There are a few minor scribal issues — a word misspelled, some misplaced punctuation, a line skipped in one manuscript because it began with the same word as the line above. When people say there are thousands of errors in the manuscripts, these are the kinds of things they're talking about.

But we have over ten thousand ancient manuscripts of the New Testament. That means that we can spot these tiny errors with ease and correct them.

Content-wise, the oldest manuscripts are identical to the newest ones. No stories evolve; no people change; no doctrines transform. The content is incredibly firm.

There were what seem to be two minor additions to the text: the last few verses in Mark 16:9–20 and the story of the woman caught in adultery in John 7:53–8:11. These two groups of verses don't appear in the earliest manuscripts and were likely added later.

And in doing so, they demonstrate how confident we are that the text hasn't changed over time.

How do they demonstrate this? It's simple: we can spot these additions easily. They aren't in the oldest manuscripts. And — because the content in the New Testament doesn't change over time — they stick out like a sore thumb.

If the text of the New Testament was constantly being edited or altered, we would have no way to tell. If the manuscripts kept changing over time, we would have no baseline to compare them to.

But because the content is so rigid, any attempted alterations can't hide. If a scribe adds a note in the margin and a later scribe accidentally slips it in the text, we can spot it immediately by comparing it to the thousands and thousands of other manuscripts that don't have that addition, and swiftly correct it.

Thus, we have incredible confidence today that when you read the words of Jesus in a well-translated Bible, you are genuinely reading the words of Jesus.

As a final note: there are, of course, plenty of people today who will try to claim that the New Testament was edited. But they do this largely on speculation and bluster. **The evidence of history is solidly on the side of the New Testament standing constant through time.**

Question 14

What is the origin of the idea of a loving God?[22]

This is a fun question to answer, as the answer is found in the same place whether you believe the Bible is true or not.

Either way, the origin of the idea of a loving God begins at the very beginning of the Bible:

> Then God said, "**Let us make humankind in our image, after our likeness.** And let them have dominion over the fish of the sea and over the birds of the heavens and over the livestock and over all the earth and over every creeping thing that creeps on the earth."
>
> **So God created man in his own image, in the image of God he created him; male and female he created them.**
>
> And God blessed them. And God said to them, "Be fruitful and multiply and fill the earth and subdue it, and have dominion over the fish of the sea and over the birds of the heavens and over every living thing that moves on the earth."
>
> And God said, "Behold, I have given you every plant yielding seed that is on the face of all the

earth, and every tree with seed in its fruit. You shall have them for food. And to every beast of the earth and to every bird of the heavens and to everything that creeps on the earth, everything that has the breath of life, I have given every green plant for food." And it was so.

And God saw everything that he had made, and behold, it was very good. (Genesis 1:26-31 ESV)

From the very first page of the Scriptures, God is loving. He creates humankind *in His image* — just as every baby is created in the image of its parents.

Compare this to every other cosmology our planet has ever produced. The Genesis account may very well pre-date the other mythologies. Yet even if it does not, it is still the origin of the idea of a loving God, because the other available cosmologies lacks the love that soaks every word in Genesis 1.

In ancient Babylon, the *Enuma Elish* describes the gods Apsu and Tiamat creating generations of gods, including Ea, who ended up killing Apsu. Tiamat sought revenge, but Marduk killed Tiamat, split her body in half, and used it to create the heavens and the earth. Later, Marduk created humanity to do the drudgery that the gods refused to do, like cultivating, harvesting, and tending flocks.

In ancient China, a cosmic egg containing Yin and Yang separated as Pan-gu emerged. He thrust the two halves apart and died. Humanity either originated as fleas on his body, or as the invention of the goddess Nuwa, who was lonely. She reportedly created a few humans laboriously from mud, who became the nobles. But they took so long to make that Nuwa simply flung mud droplets to create the mass of commoners.

In ancient India, the Rig Veda describes the enormous Purusha enveloping the entire world. The other gods killed Purusha. Birds and animals appeared from his corpse, along with the four castes of society: the priests, the warriors, the commoners, and the servants.

All of these stories lack love.

The closest to love is Nuwa, who laboriously fashions the noble caste. Yet she thinks little of the commoners, flinging them out carelessly.

Only in the Bible does a loving God create *all of humanity* in His image — female and male, old and young, every ethnicity that will ever exist.

Yet the contrast is even starker compared to modern mythologies.

In modern naturalism, no one creates humanity. We arise by accident, out of inorganic material that has no significance. No one cares that we exist, and no one will care if we all go extinct.

There's no trace of love in such a concept of humanity's origin. Nor is there much science; the study of how life could arise from non-life has produced dead end after dead end. The more we study it, the more impossible it seems.

To put it differently: **Every other ancient cosmology succumbs to the folly of pride.**

Gods kill each other. Humanity is created to do drudgery, because the gods don't want to do it themselves. Some humans receive care; others are flung carelessly. In all of these creation stories, the gods are so full of pride and self-concern that humanity is mostly an afterthought.

Only in the Bible does God create through love, for the purpose of building humanity up.

God creates a lavish paradise, lovingly crafting every segment bit-by-bit. Once it's ready, He fashions humanity in the grandest possible way — in His own image.

Then, in true love, He gives: God hands the world over to humanity to rule.

On top of that, God seeks a personal relationship with each human being, walking with Adam and Eve in the cool of the day, talking and loving and enjoying each other's presence.

To circle back to the question: Where did the idea of a loving God originate?

With the God of the Bible, who lovingly created humanity as His children, in His image.

This same God demonstrated His love for His children by laying His life down on the Cross, suffering in our place so that we could enter into a loving relationship with Him.

This is God. This is Jesus. This is love.

Question 15

Why were the four canonical gospels written so long after Christ's death and resurrection?[23]

They weren't. **The four Gospels were written by eye-witnesses or their scribes.**

To prove this, we only have to look to history.

Many people today disagree about who wrote the Gospels and when, but history does not. I'll quote much of what the ancient historians themselves record about how each Gospel came to be, so that you can examine the evidence yourself.

The quick summary:

- **Matthew**, an eye-witness of Jesus' life and ministry, wrote his Gospel first, in the 40's or 50's.

- **Mark** wrote second, recording the oral testimony of Peter, one of Jesus' closest disciples, in the 50's or early 60's.

- **Luke** wrote third, no later than 68, recording the eye-witness testimony of a wide crowd of people.

- **John** wrote last, in the 90's, being perhaps Jesus' closest friend on earth and an eye-witness to more than any other disciple.

History establishes all of this.

You'll notice that many who scoff at the Scriptures ignore these historical references completely. They'll argue that the Gospels were written anonymously, or that they were written late by a school of students, or that they changed over time. But whenever they make these claims they ignore history. They have to. History destroys such arguments.

Matthew

History unanimously records Matthew as the first Gospel. Matthew, one of Jesus' twelve disciples, wrote down the life of Jesus early on in the first century, so that the early church would have a definitive record of what Jesus did and said.

Again, many today will disagree with those statements. But we have only to look to history to find the proof.

Papias (ca. 60–130, *Fragments of Papias*):

> "Matthew put together the oracles [of the Lord] in the Hebrew style, and each one interpreted them as best he could."

It's short, but powerful, particularly because it's our earliest witness. It establishes that Matthew himself is the author of his Gospel, that he wrote in the Hebrew style (meaning either in the Hebrew language itself, or in Greek, but in a Hebrew manner of speech), and that the early church used it widely as their authority.

Irenaeus (ca. 130–200; *Against Heresies* 3.1.1–2; cf. Eusebius, *Ecclesiastical History* 5.8.1–4):

> **"So Matthew brought out a written gospel among the Jews in their own style, when Peter and Paul were preaching the gospel at Rome and founding the church.** But after their demise Mark himself, the disciple and recorder of Peter, has also handed on to us in writing what had been proclaimed by Peter. And Luke, the follower of Paul, set forth in a book the gospel that was proclaimed by him. Later John, the disciple of the Lord and the one who leaned against his chest, also put out a Gospel while residing in Ephesus of Asia."

Matthew thus publishes his Gospel sometime in the late 40's or early 50's in the first century. Tradition is unanimous that Peter died a martyr's death in Rome during the persecution of Nero, which he unleashed from 54-68 A.D./C.E.

Despite being one of our earliest records, this Irenaeus' statement contains most of what skeptics think arose "late." Note all that it establishes: Matthew wrote his Gospel first, while Peter and Paul were both preaching, making it incredibly early; Mark wrote his Gospel second, recording the speeches of Peter; Luke wrote his Gospel as he followed Paul; John wrote his Gospel last while he lived in Ephesus.

Those who argue that the Gospels were written anonymously have to answer why the earliest historical records clearly establish the authors.

Mark

Mark is a fun one. He's easily the most widely-talked about in the historical record.

Mark did not set out to write a Gospel, but he was simply in the right place at the right time. Peter gave a series of lectures in Rome, which the audience loved so much they asked Mark to record them in print. We refer to those notes today as the Gospel of Mark.

Like Matthew, the Gospel of Mark had to be written and published before Nero's persecution concluded, as it claimed Peter's life. Mark can thus be safely assigned a date in the 50's or early 60's, at the latest.

Again, just check the history:

Clement of Alexandria (ca. 150–215; *Adumbrationes in Epistolas Canonicas* on 1 Peter 5:13):

> "Mark, the follower of Peter, while Peter was publicly preaching the gospel at Rome in the presence of some of Caesar's knights and uttering many testimonies about Christ, on their asking him to let them have a record of the things that had been said, wrote the Gospel that is called the Gospel of Mark from the things said by Peter, just as Luke is recognized as the pen that wrote the Acts of the Apostles and as the translator of the Letter of Paul to the Hebrews."

This is expanded and explained in the Old Latin Prologue to Mark (recension 2; second century):

> "...Mark, who was also called Stubfinger because he had shorter fingers with regard to the other dimensions of the body. He had been the disciple and recorder of Peter, whom he followed, just as he had heard him relating. **Having been asked by the brethren in Rome, he wrote this short Gospel in the regions of Italy. When Peter heard about it, he approved and authorized it to be read to the church with [his own] authority.** But after the demise of Peter, taking this Gospel that he had composed he journeyed to Egypt, and being ordained the first bishop of Alexandria he founded the church there, preaching Christ. He was a man of such great learning and austerity of life that he induced all the followers of Christ to imitate his example. Last of all John, perceiving that the external facts had been made plain in the Gospel,

and being urged by his friends and inspired by the Spirit, composed a spiritual Gospel."

The following again corroborates what the first two establish:

Eusebius (ca. 260–340; *Ecclesiastical History* 2.15.1–16.1):

> "To such a degree did the flame of true piety illuminate the minds of Peter's hearers that, not being satisfied with having just one hearing or with the unwritten teaching of the divine proclamation, **with every sort of entreaty they urged Mark, whose Gospel it is reputed to be, being the follower of Peter, to bequeath to them also in writing the record of the teaching handed on to them by word [of mouth], nor did they let up before convincing the man. And by this means they became the cause of the Gospel writing that is said to be 'according to Mark.'** They also say that when the apostle learned what had happened, the Spirit having revealed this to him, he was pleased with the enthusiasm of the men and authorized the writing for reading in the churches. Clement in the sixth book of *The Outlines* relates the story, and the bishop of Hierapolis, Papias by name, bears joint witness to him. He also says that Peter mentions Mark in his First Letter, and that he composed this in Rome itself, which they say that he himself indicates, speaking figuratively of the city of Babylon, by

these words: 'The Elect [Lady] in Babylon greets you, along with Mark my son.' Now they say that this Mark was the first to be sent to Egypt to preach the gospel that he had also committed to writing, and was the first to establish churches in Alexandria itself."

Eusebius refers to Papias' testimony, which we also happen to have:

"This too the Elder used to say: **Mark, having become the recorder of Peter, indeed wrote accurately albeit not in order whatever he [Peter] remembered of the things either said or done by the Lord.** For he [Mark] had neither heard the Lord nor was a follower of him, but later, as I said, of Peter, who used to deliver his teachings in the form of short stories, but not making as it were a literary composition of the Lord's sayings, so that Mark did not err at all when he wrote down certain things just as he [Peter] recalled them. **For he had but one intention: not to leave out anything he had heard nor to falsify anything in them.**"

Luke

Luke is a unique Gospel, in that much of its composition can be deduced from the words Luke wrote. He states openly in the first four verses of the Gospel of Luke that he was not an eye-witness, but he extensively interviewed those who were. He composed this work for the benefit of Theophilus, that he can have certainty about the things he has been taught. One of Luke's primary eye-witnesses was Mary, the mother of Jesus, as Luke's Gospel tells many of her personal stories.

History again corroborates Luke's authenticity, beginning with its status as the third Gospel written, as the Anti-Marcionite Prologue to Luke (second century) testifies:

> "There were already Gospels in existence, that according to Matthew, written down in Judea, and that according to Mark in Italy. **But guided by the Holy Spirit, he [Luke] composed in the regions around Achaia the whole of the Gospel.**"

Origin establishes that Luke was written for a Gentile audience, and that Paul particularly praised Luke, perhaps because Paul spent so much time reaching out to Gentiles.

Origen (ca. 185–254; quoted in Eusebius, *Ecclesiastical History* 6.25.3–6):

> "[Origen] testifies that he knows only four Gospels. . . . The first written was that according to the onetime tax collector but later apostle of Jesus Christ, Matthew, who published it for the believers from Judaism, composed in Hebrew characters. And second, that according to Mark, composed as Peter guided. . . . **And third, that according to Luke, the Gospel praised by Paul, composed for those**

from the Gentiles. After them all, that according to John."

Given that Luke wrote while following Paul, and that Paul died no later than 68 A.D./C.E. in Rome, we can safely assign the Gospel of Luke a date in the early-to-mid 60's.

John

Among the four Gospels, John is subject to the most skepticism. Few critical scholars accept that the Apostle John wrote the Gospel of John. Yet the curious thing is this: every fragment of the historical witness assigns the Gospel to John the Apostle. Those who doubt this do so against every possible piece of historical evidence.

Let's examine a couple:

Tertullian (ca. 160–225; Against Marcion 4.2.1–2):

> "I lay it down to begin with that the documents of the gospel have the apostles for their authors, and that this task of promulgating the gospel was imposed upon them by the Lord himself. . . . In short, **from among the apostles, John and Matthew implant in us the faith**, while from among the apostolic men Luke and Mark reaffirm it."

The Muratorian Fragment, from the second century):

> "At which, however, he [Mark] was present and has thus stated. In the third place, the book of the Gospel according to Luke... **The fourth of the Gospels is John's, one of the disciples.**"

And again, from the Old Latin Prologue to Mark, from the second century:

> "Last of all John, perceiving that the external facts had been made plain in the Gospel, and being urged by his friends and inspired by the Spirit, composed a spiritual Gospel."

John's publication is the most widely accepted among the critical community, with most agreeing it was composed and published in the late 90's of the first century.

All the Other "Gospels"

Some today claim that there were many other Gospels competing with Matthew, Mark, Luke, and John. But this again goes against all the available evidence.

The other "Gospels" we have are not true Gospels at all. None come anywhere close to the length of the Four, nor do they attempt to do the same thing: to narrate the life and ministry of Jesus.

Even from the beginning, they were recognized as the products of fringe sects, writing short documents to back up their divergent theology. The testimony from history is unanimous. Origen provides a good summary:

Origen (ca. 185–254; Homilies on Luke 1):

> "For Matthew did not 'take in hand' but wrote by the Holy Spirit, and so did Mark and John and also equally Luke. . . . For there is also the gospel 'according to Thomas,' and that 'according to Matthias,' and many others. These are the ones 'that have been taken in hand.' But the church of God accepts only the four."

After looking at history, we can comfortably say who wrote the Gospels, who was an eye-witness, and when they wrote:

Matthew: A personal eye-witness to most of Jesus' ministry. He wrote very early, in the 40's or 50's.

Mark: He recorded the testimony of Peter, a direct eye-witness for most of Jesus' ministry. Mark wrote no later than 64, and likely earlier, when it was safe for Peter to lecture publicly in Rome.

Luke: While Luke was not an eye-witness, he conducted extensive research, recording the personal testimonies of many eye-witnesses, including Jesus' mother Mary. Luke wrote no later than 68,

John: The longest-living eye-witness of Jesus wrote his Gospel in the 90's, filling out the story with details the other three Gospels didn't include.

Many will contend with this answer. Yet all I've done is recite the witness of history and summarize it. If anyone disagrees with this, pay attention to their reasoning. They will have no historical evidence to deny these claims, because history is entirely on the side of the authenticity of the Gospels.

Question 16

Isn't it unfair to Jesus that the three main branches of Christianity claim to derive their divine mandate from Him as God, although He said: 'Why callest thou me good, none is good except the Father'?[24]

This is a great question. It gives us an excellent example of the brilliance of Jesus' teaching.

Let's take the pieces of this question in reverse.

First, we need to clarify the statement Jesus actually made. Three Gospels record it for us (See Matthew 19:17, Mark 10:18, Luke 18:19). I'll use a more modern translation, as the King James quoted above is so archaic its meaning can get lost.

> Jesus said to him, "Why do you call me good? No one is good except God alone." (Mark 10:18 ESV)

What did Jesus mean by this?

The surrounding passages give us the framework to see exactly what Jesus was getting at.

A young man raced up to Jesus and knelt before Him. He was eager to see Jesus. A question had been burning in his heart, so he asks, "*Good Teacher, what must I do to inherit eternal life?*"

Jesus could have responded with a few points of data, saying you must do X, Y, and Z to live eternally. But first, Jesus wants to expose this man's heart. The question sounds good, but Jesus needed to reveal what was prompting this question and how receptive the man truly was to receiving the answer.

So Jesus employs one of the most brilliant conversational tactics: He answers a question with a question.

Jesus asks: "*WHY* do you call Me good? No one is good except God."

Does the man call Jesus good simply because Jesus is a popular teacher?

Does he call Jesus good to flatter Jesus?

Does he call Jesus good because he likes Jesus' moral teaching?

Or does he call Jesus good because he believes Jesus is God?

If the man answers with any of the former three options, then he won't be able to hear Jesus' answer. If Jesus gives an answer the man does not like, then these three options give him a reason to walk away. Perhaps Jesus was popular, but not always right; perhaps Jesus can't be flattered into giving a favorable answer; perhaps Jesus only knows good morality and His answers on the afterlife are lacking.

The only way the man will listen to Jesus' answer is if he truly believes Jesus is God. If he calls Jesus "Good" because he believes Jesus is God, then he has to listen to Jesus' answer, because there is no other place to go for that answer.

But if the man does not see Jesus as God — if he sees Jesus merely as a skilled teacher or philosopher — then he has room to disagree with Jesus and turn to go somewhere else for an answer.

After setting the stage this way, Jesus continues:

> "You know the commandments: 'Do not murder, Do not commit adultery, Do not steal, Do not bear false witness, Do not defraud, Honor your father and mother.'"
>
> And he said to him, "Teacher, all these I have kept from my youth."
>
> And Jesus, looking at him, loved him, and said to him, "You lack one thing: go, sell all that you have and give to the poor, and you will have treasure in heaven; and come, follow me." (Mark 10:19-21 ESV)

It is interesting to note that the young man dropped the word "good" when he addressed Jesus the second time. After Jesus put the spotlight on why the man called Jesus "good," the man backed away from using the word. This implies that he isn't entirely sure why he used it, or that he isn't comfortable using it as Jesus desires. Jesus was clear: only call Me "good" if you believe that I'm God. And the man stopped calling Jesus "good."

In other words: he doesn't believe Jesus is God.

He demonstrates this clearly in his response:

> Disheartened by the saying, he went away sorrowful, for he had great possessions. (Mark 10:22 ESV)

If he believed Jesus to be God, he would have listened, because only the God who created the afterlife can give you entrance into it.

Instead, he walks away. He doesn't like Jesus' answer, so he leaves. He'll go find an answer he likes better, an answer that lets him keep all his wealth.

At this point, some may object and ask, "But wasn't Jesus refusing to be identified with God?"

Reading the rest of Mark sheds all light on this that we need.

Throughout Mark (and every Gospel) Jesus is constantly identifying Himself as God. He does this in a wide variety of ways: He fulfills prophecies left and right, He performs more miracles than all the books in the world could describe, He teaches with authority no one else possesses, and on the list goes. Jesus makes the case in every possible way that He truly is God.

But let's look at one piece of evidence in particular: **Jesus does what only God can do — forgive sins.**

> And when [Jesus] returned to Capernaum after some days, it was reported that he was at home. And many were gathered together, so that there was no more room, not even at the door. And he was preaching the word to them.
>
> And they came, bringing to him a paralytic carried by four men. And when they could not get near him because of the crowd, they removed the roof above him, and when they had made an opening, they let down the bed on which the paralytic lay.
>
> And when Jesus saw their faith, he said to the paralytic, "**Son, your sins are forgiven.**"
>
> Now some of the scribes were sitting there, questioning in their hearts, "Why does this man speak like that? He is blaspheming! **Who can forgive sins but God alone?**"
>
> And immediately Jesus, perceiving in his spirit that they thus questioned within themselves, said to

them, "Why do you question these things in your hearts? Which is easier, to say to the paralytic, 'Your sins are forgiven,' or to say, 'Rise, take up your bed and walk'? But that you may know that the Son of Man has authority on earth to forgive sins"- he said to the paralytic- "I say to you, rise, pick up your bed, and go home."

And he rose and immediately picked up his bed and went out before them all, so that they were all amazed and glorified God, saying, "We never saw anything like this!" (Mark 2:1-12, ESV)

The scribes were correct: only God can forgive sins. If Jesus is claiming to forgive sins, He is claiming to be God. They interpreted this (wrongly) as blasphemy, thinking that a mere man was sullying the name of God by claiming to be God.

And Jesus doesn't correct them.

He *wants* them to make the connection that forgiving sins is claiming to be God. That was His entire point!

Jesus then doubles down on this by healing the paralytic in front of them all, demonstrating that He wasn't simply speaking the words, "Your sins are forgiven." By healing the paralytic, Jesus demonstrated that He has full divine power to heal, which means Jesus also has full divine power to forgive.

Which means that Jesus is God.

Some of you may respond as the scribes did. They heard this and rejected it in their hearts, refusing to believe that any human person could be God. They did not consider what the evidence declared. They only considered what they wanted to believe, and so they rejected the clear miracle in front of their eyes.

I urge you: *look at the evidence.*

Jesus made incredible claims — that He was God come in the flesh to redeem us back to Him.

But He backed up those incredible claims with evidence, because He wanted to give us every possible chance to believe.

Look at the evidence.

Jesus is good.

Because Jesus is God.

To return to the original question, we need to answer this:

"Isn't it most unfair to Jesus that the three main branches of Christianity claim to derive their divine mandate from Him as God, although He said: 'Why calmest thou me good, none is good except the Father?'"

Based on what Jesus taught about Himself — no, it's not unfair.

The three main branches of Christianity believe that Jesus is God because Jesus claimed to be God and proved it time and time again.

This is why the four Gospels were written: to preserve this evidence and pass it along to every future generation.

Question 17

Why was God mad at Adam and Eve for eating the apple and becoming knowledgeable?[25]

That's not why God became angry.

Adam and Eve were knowledgeable before the Tree. They had immense knowledge of everything good.

But when they ate the forbidden fruit, they gained the knowledge of evil. *That's* **what God hated.**

Before the Fall, God enjoyed perfect intimacy with Adam and Eve. He loved them and they loved Him. God delighted to provide for every need they had. He literally designed a perfect Paradise for them.

When they introduced evil to this world, God mourned. He loves His children. He wants intimacy with them. He's angry when that intimacy is shattered, as anyone would be.

Imagine if you raised your child extremely well and had a beautiful relationship with them. But one day they tell you they joined a cult and have to cut off all communication with you.

What would you feel? Anger? Betrayal? Sadness?

That's what God felt when His children chose the path that led to death after He did everything possible to keep them on the path that leads to life.

But God loves His kids.

He didn't abandon Adam and Eve. He stayed with them. They still spoke daily. He still pursued their hearts. But part of their intimacy was gone, now. They could never be as close to God as before, because they had chosen to know evil as well as good.

But God won't let evil win.

God came in the flesh to die on a Cross to remove the penalty for evil once and for all. He did it because He loves His kids and He wants intimacy restored.

That's what He invites us to.

Question 18

How does the Christian belief in the resurrection provide a resource for dealing with and understanding suffering?[26]

Jesus' Resurrection means that all suffering will end — and joy can replace it.

Suffering is real, and it's universal. Jesus suffered. That simple statement proves a powerful point: *everyone* suffers.

Jesus lived a perfect life, perfectly trusted God, and perfectly accomplished everything He was supposed to do. Yet He suffered more agony than anyone else. If He suffered, then we all will. And if Jesus suffered, despite pleasing God perfectly, then we can know that our suffering is not because God is mad at us.

Suffering is real.

But it's also on its way out.

Jesus rose from death. That means that death is not the end. Suffering is not the end. Pain is not the end.

They are all defeated by *life*.

Death could not hold Jesus. He rose, more alive than anyone has ever been. He bore scars, *but they had no power over him*. He could joyfully display them, freed of pain and shame.

Jesus' Resurrection proves that death will die, suffering will slip away, and pain will never win. It can't. **Life will outlive pain.**

Whenever you suffer, you can look to Jesus for reassurance that this suffering will pass. It will not destroy you. You will outlive it. You will survive, but your pain will not.

If you follow Christ, then suffering can't beat you. In Christ, you will outlive death. Pain will become a distant memory.

Even while we live on this earth, pain loses its power. It still hurts. But God can use everything in life — even pain — and bring good out of it.

Jesus' Cross is the prime example. He suffered more intense pain than we can ever imagine. But through that pain God delivered us from hellfire. The Crucifixion was the evilest act in history, a truly innocent man killed in the place of His killers — and God brought about the greatest good from it.

Jesus' Resurrection means that life wins. Love wins. Peace wins. God wins.

If you are in Christ, there will come a day when you are so *alive* that your worst pain today will be less than a bad dream, fading away until forgotten.

Jesus' Resurrection means that you will truly *live*.

Question 19

Was there an eclipse when Jesus was crucified?[27]

Yes.

Not only was there a lunar eclipse during Jesus' crucifixion, but there was also a three-hour long darkness that covered much of the world.

But let's back up a second.

The darkness at the time of Jesus' Crucifixion gives us solid proof — either of the Bible lying or the Bible recording a remarkable truth. The Bible describes two spectacular events on the day of Jesus' Crucifixion.

Listen to how Mark describes the first: "And when the sixth hour had come, **there was darkness over the whole land** until the ninth hour" (Mark 15:33, NIV).

If darkness covered the entire land, it would be visible to more than those in Jerusalem. Everybody around the Roman Empire should have seen *something*, if it was real.

The second event likewise would be visible everywhere. Joel prophesied it and Peter quoted it:

"This is what was spoken about through the prophet Joel: [...] 'I will perform wonders in the sky above [...] **The sun will be changed to darkness and the moon to blood** before the great and glorious day of the Lord comes. And then everyone who calls on the name of the Lord will be saved.' [...] Jesus the Nazarene, a man clearly attested to you by God with powerful deeds, wonders, and **miraculous signs** that God performed among you through him, **just as you yourselves know.**" (Acts 2:16, 19–22 NET)

A blood moon occurs during a lunar eclipse. As with the darkness, it should be widely visible, if indeed it happened during Jesus' crucifixion — as Peter indicates it did.

If we find nothing in the historical record, then it appears the Bible lied.

But do find this in the historical record — well, then things get interesting.

So what do we find?

Thallus was one of the first to write about the darkness at the time of the Crucifixion, writing at about 52 AD/CE. His original work has been lost, but Julius Africanus, an historian who wrote around 221 A.D., quotes Thallus to disagree with him:

> **'On the whole world there pressed a most fearful darkness**; and the rocks were rent by an earthquake, and many places in Judea and other districts were thrown down. This darkness Thallus, in the third book of his History, calls, as appears to me without reason, an eclipse of the sun.'

Both of Thallus and Julius attest to the darkness as a real event, so much so that they can bicker about the cause.

Phlegon, a Greek historian and author of a detailed chronology in 137 AD/CE, wrote:

> "In the fourth year of the 202nd Olympiad (33 AD/CE) there was '**the greatest eclipse of the sun**' and that '**it became night in the sixth hour of the day [noon] so that stars even appeared in the heavens**. There was a great earthquake in Bithynia, and many things were overturned in Nicaea.'"

This one is especially handy, as it corroborates the exact year and time of day for the darkness, as well as and the earthquake.

Africanus also wrote a five-volume history of the world c. 221 AD/CE. His account is particularly noteworthy both for its length and for his credibility; he had impressed Roman Emperor Alexander Severus so well with his historical rigor that he was put in charge of the Emperor's library in the Pantheon; in other words, he was the most well-known, influential, and well-resourced historian in the Empire.

While I quoted him briefly above to highlight Thallus' contribution, Africanus' full paragraph adds a great deal more detail:

> "On the whole world there pressed a most fearful darkness; and the rocks were rent by an earthquake, and many places in Judea and other districts were thrown down. This darkness Thallus, in the third book of his History, calls, as appears to me without reason, an eclipse of the sun. For the Hebrews celebrate the passover on the 14th day according to the moon, and the passion of our Savior falls on the day before the passover; but an eclipse of the sun takes place only when the moon comes under the sun. And it cannot happen at any other time but in the interval between the first day of the new moon and the last of the old, that is, at their junction: how then should an eclipse be supposed to happen when the moon is almost diametrically opposite the sun? Let opinion pass however; let it carry the majority with it; and let this portent of the world be deemed an eclipse of the sun, like others a portent only to the eye. Phlegon records that, in the time of Tiberius Caesar, at full moon, **there was a full eclipse of the sun from the sixth hour to the ninth**—manifestly that one of which we speak. But what has an eclipse in common with an earthquake, the rending rocks, and the resurrection of the dead, and so great a perturbation throughout the universe? Surely no such event as this is recorded for a long period."

This one additionally is valuable given that it mentions the resurrection of the dead and again the earthquake, in addition to the darkness.

Tertullian (second century) also provides a remarkable attestation, writing:

> "**At the moment of Christ's death, the light departed from the sun, and the land was darkened at noonday**, which wonder is related in your own annals, and is preserved in your archives to this day."

Not only does Tertullian attest to it, but he appeals to how well-recorded the event is in established historical archives of the time. This is perhaps the most significant attribution, given that he cites how extensively the event was recorded and appeals to the public records to prove his point.

The darkness, then, is well-established.

What do we find about a blood moon?

It turns out that a lunar eclipse did happen *on exactly the day the darkness was recorded*: April 3, 33 A.D./C.E.

With modern astronomy software, we can rewind the sky and verify exactly what this lunar eclipse looked like. NASA provides the information clearly:

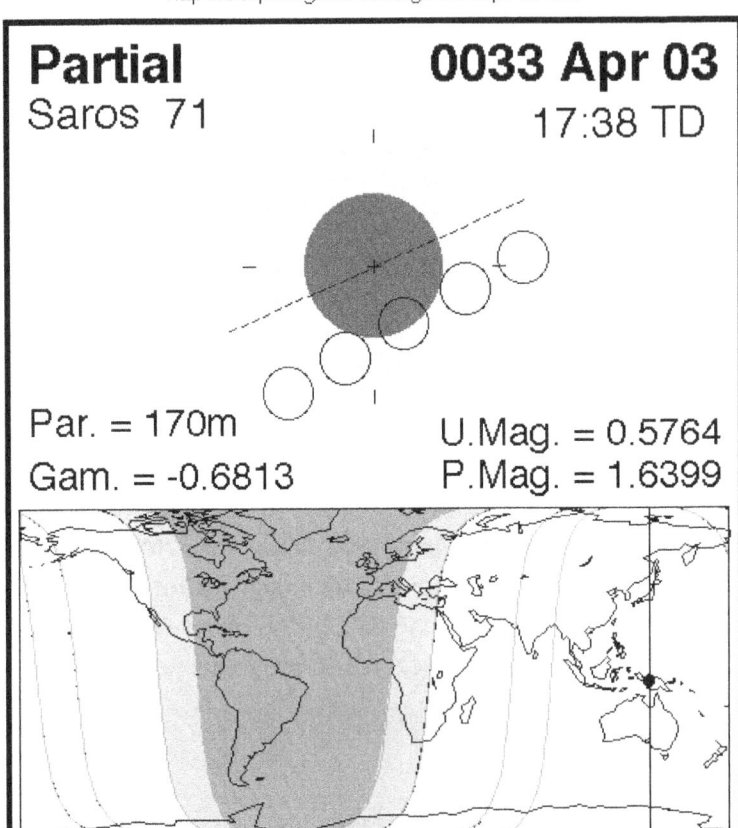

```
Partial                    0033 Apr 03
Saros 71                        17:38 TD

Par. = 170m                U.Mag. = 0.5764
Gam. = -0.6813             P.Mag. = 1.6399
```

http://eclipse.gsfc.nasa.gov/eclipse.html

Five Millennium Canon of Lunar Eclipses (Espenak & Meeus)
NASA TP-2009-214172

The precise data on the partial lunar eclipses of April 3, 33 A.D./C.E.

Peter knew his audience had witnessed this blood moon. He connected this fulfillment with the specific prophecy that looked forward to it hundreds of years in advance. Again, as Acts records:

"This is what was spoken about through the prophet Joel: [...] 'I will perform wonders in the sky above [...] **The sun will be changed to darkness and the moon to blood** before the great and glorious day of the Lord comes. And then everyone who calls on the name of the Lord will be saved.' [...] Jesus the Nazarene, a man clearly attested to you by God with powerful deeds, wonders, and **miraculous signs** that God performed among you through him, **just as you yourselves know.**" (Acts 2:16, 19–22 NET)

It is true, as the Psalms say, that *"The heavens declare the glory of God!"* (Psalm 19:1) The Crucifixion of Jesus is recorded not only in Scripture and history, but in the very motion of the sun, moon, and Earth.

A view of the partial lunar eclipse on August 7, 2017 as seen from Malta in the Mediterranean Sea. Credit and copyright: Leonard Ellul-Mercer.

Consider what this means! From the moment God spun our solar system into place, He ordained the motion of the planets such that at the precise moment Jesus would perish on the Cross, our planet would begin eclipsing the Moon, turning its light to blood.

God set this story in place in the heavens from ancient days. Peter's audience witnessed it – and now, so can we.

Skeptics have long scoffed at these details in the Bible. But like most details in the Scriptures, when you dig into the research, you find the claims verified.

The Bible is not a book of cleverly-invented myths. It records real events that happened in real history. The more we press into the individual details, the more we find them verified.

Question 20

Why do I think thoughts that I'm opposed to thinking? Could the devil be speaking deceptive messages to me?[28]

This is a fascinating question. I'll give a brief answer as best I can.

But for a far more detailed and complete answer, I recommend the book *Christ-Centered Therapy*, by Neil Anderson, Terry Zuehlke, and Julie Zuehlke.

The beauty of this book is the way it combines the physical, mental, and spiritual to form a complete picture of a human being. Each author brings their unique expertise. As per its description: "Christ-Centered Therapy unites the wisdom and expertise of pastoral theologian and best-selling author Dr. Neil Anderson (Doctorate of Ministry) and professional Christian counselors Dr. Terry (Ph.D) and Julianne Zuehlke (M.S.)."[29]

This book will answer your original question, along with a great deal of further questions you're likely to have as you keep exploring these topics.

That's the long answer.

113

To provide the short answer, let's break this down.

Why do we think thoughts that we are opposed to thinking?

First, let me say: you're not alone. Everyone struggles with this.

Second, you're in very good company, as a Christian asking this question. The Apostle Paul expressed the same frustration, about his thoughts but also about his actions:

> I don't understand what I am doing. For I do not do what I want—instead, I do what I hate. [...] For I want to do the good, but I cannot do it. For I do not do the good I want, but I do the very evil I do not want! (Romans 7:15–19 NET)

Not only did Paul think thoughts he was opposed to thinking, but he performed actions he was opposed to doing, and found himself doing it continually. (And if we're honest, I think every human would say we all do the same thing).

Third, let's talk about where these thoughts come from.

In short: they can come from anywhere. Other people, your own ruminations, ads you see on TV, teachers from school, a random character's words from a movie you watched five years ago, or yes, from demons.

So, to answer the last part of the question: *Could the devil be involved in having deceptive messages and past conditioning?*

Yes — but that doesn't mean much.

Here's the key: the devil can't make you do anything, even if he does put thoughts in your mind. **You control you.** The choice is always yours as to whether you will listen to your thoughts, reject them, or replace them with better thoughts.

Paul struggled with this same mental battle, so he knows how to fight. He provides great wisdom:

> Finally, brothers, whatever is true, whatever is honorable, whatever is just, whatever is pure, whatever is lovely, whatever is commendable, if there is any excellence, if there is anything worthy of praise, think about these things. (Philippians 4:8)

It seems simple — think good thoughts.

But it works.

Let me give you a quick example: **stress**. A man I work with felt God calling him to eliminate a lot of the noise in his daily life. He cut out watching the news, reading random things on the internet, music that had depressing lyrics, etc. He even took a few solitude retreats to sit in silence with no external stimulation.

He found an amazing thing: peace returned to him. He hadn't realized how stressed and anxious he was until he felt peace again. He hadn't felt that way in years.

Our culture is louder than ever. We have near-constant stimulation. Everyone is shouting at us and their words get stuck inside our minds, even when you try to ignore them.

So take a break from it.

Cut out the noise for a few weeks. In its place, simply read the Bible. Let its messages be loudest voice in your life for a few weeks.

I promise: you will notice a drastic change in your thought life and your emotions.

Question 21

How do we know how the apostles died? Is there evidence? [30]

To take these in reverse:

Is there evidence?

Yes — abundantly and from a wide variety of sources, including secular historians, letters between church fathers, Gnostic sources, pseudopigraphical sources, and the New Testament itself.

Naturally, there is more evidence concerning the primary Apostles — Peter, James, Paul — than for the others. Yet all are attested to in some fashion.

A Quora answer is too short a space to examine all the details, but I can point you to a fantastic compilation and analysis of all the available evidence. Sean McDowell wrote a 469 page dissertation entitled "A Historical Evaluation of the Evidence for the Death of the Apostles as Martyrs For Their Faith."[31]

The entire report is fascinating, but I'll quote the conclusion to provide a concise answer to the first part of the original question: *How do we know how the apostles died?*

The willingness of the apostles to suffer and die for their faith is a critical step in establishing their sincerity and reliability as the first witnesses to the risen Jesus. This section will contain summaries of key findings and draw some general conclusions from this investigation. These initial points portray the context, which provides a general expectation for the martyrdom of the apostles. The final section includes summary findings of the individual apostles and draws some final conclusions.

Summary of the Contextual Evidence

Six points stand out as most relevant for this investigation.

First, the Christian movement was a resurrection movement since its inception. To believe in Jesus was to believe that he had risen from the grave, conquering death and sin. There is no evidence the earliest Christians considered the resurrection secondary. This is clear from the centrality of the resurrection in the earliest creeds, which predate the writing of the New Testament books (e.g., Rom 1:3-4; 4:24b-25; 1 Thess 4:14; 1 Cor 15:3-7). The resurrection also held central place in the apostolic kerygma as represented in the sermon summaries in Acts (e.g. Acts 2:24). From the earliest records of the Christian faith to the writings of the Apostolic Fathers, it is evident the apostles had a resurrection faith.

Second, the twelve apostles were the first witnesses to the resurrection and they launched the initial missionary movement from Jerusalem. The missionary efforts of the apostles are supported by both internal and external evidence. They had been with Jesus at least from his baptism until the ascension, and they were eyewitnesses of Jesus after his death (Acts 1:21-22). Paul and James the brother of the Lord were not members of the Twelve, but they were eyewitnesses of the resurrection (1 Cor 15:7-8) who were willing to suffer and die for their beliefs. After Pentecost, the apostles boldly proclaimed that Jesus is the risen Messiah, even though they were threatened, persecuted, thrown in jail, and martyred (Acts 4:1-22; 5:18-32; 7:54-60; 12:2).

Third, Christians were persecuted in the early church. Jesus had predicted his followers would be persecuted (Matt 10:16-23; Mark 13:9; John 15:18-27; 16:2-3, 33) and that they would suffer and die like Israel had done to the prophets (Matt 21:33-40; 22:6; 23:30-31, 34, 37; Mark 12:1-11; Luke 6:22-23; 11:47-50; 13:34; 20:9-18). Paul not only suffered deeply for proclaiming the gospel (2 Cor 6:4-9), he also taught that Christians should expect to suffer as well (Rom 8:35-36; 1 Thess 3:3-4; Phil 1:29; 2 Tim 4:5). The expectation of persecution and suffering is a central theme throughout the entirety of the New Testament. Specifically, persecution began with the Jews, as reported in the book of Acts. They turned Jesus over to face crucifixion and threatened, beat, and killed some of the first Christians (Acts 4:13-22; 5:40; 7:54-60). Roman persecution began during the reign of Nero. He was the first emperor to use state power against Christians. Once Christians were officially condemned for the name by Nero, nothing would prevent other provincial governors from persecuting Christians in their districts for their "deviant" behavior. Christians were largely persecuted for three reasons including that they followed a crucified "criminal," practiced seemingly bizarre rituals, and refused to pay homage to the Roman gods.

Fourth, although there is not early evidence each of the apostles died as martyrs, some general claims make their deaths more likely than not. For instance, in his Letter to the Philippians 9, Polycarp places "other apostles" in the same category as Ignatius and Paul, who were known martyrs. Fourth century Syrian Father Aphrahat referred to "(others) of the apostles hereafter in diverse places confessed and proved true martyrs."[1]

Fifth, the apostles were willing to suffer and die for their faith. The apostles begin healing the sick and proclaiming Christ at Pentecost. The consistent reason they gave is that Jesus appeared to them personally over a lengthy period of time (Acts 1:3). They were threatened, beaten, thrown in prison, and killed for their faith, and yet they refused to back down because they felt the necessity to obey God rather than men (Acts 5:29). Whether or not all the apostles actually died as martyrs, they all willingly proclaimed the risen Jesus with full knowledge it could cost them their lives.

Sixth, there are no accounts that any of the apostles recanted their faith. If any of the apostles were known to have abandoned their faith under pressure, the enemies of the church would have seized this opportunity to discount the burgeoning movement. And yet there is not a single account that any of the Twelve, including Paul and James, recanted their belief that Jesus had appeared to them alive after his death. This is not insignificant evidence for the martyrdom of the apostles.

The Individual Apostles

As for the individual apostles, the historical evidence leads to the following assessments regarding the likelihood of their martyrdoms:

1. Peter: the highest possible probability

2. Paul: the highest possible probability

3. James, brother of Jesus: very probably true

4. John, the son of Zebedee: improbable

5. Thomas: more probable than not

6. Andrew: more probable than not

7. James, son of Zebedee: highest possible probability

8. Philip: possible

9. Bartholomew: more possible than not

10. Matthew: possible

11. James, son of Alphaeus: more possible than not

12. Thaddeus: possible

13. Simon the Zealot: possible

14. Matthias: possible

In sum, there are three apostles in the category of highest possible probability, one that is very probably true, two that are more probable than not, two that are more possible than not, five that are possible, and one that is improbable. Thus, of the fourteen apostles, eight are at least more possible than not, five are possible and only one is lower than possible (John). More evidence may arise someday that would alter these findings, but currently these are the most reasonable conclusions.

The willingness of the apostles to suffer and die for their faith is an important piece of the resurrection argument. It alone does not prove the resurrection is true, but it does show the apostles sincerely believed it. They were not liars. As Blaise

Pascal once said, "I only believe histories whose witnesses are ready to be put to death" (822).2 The apostles proclaimed the risen Jesus to skeptical and antagonistic audiences with full knowledge they would likely suffer and die for their beliefs. All the apostles suffered and were "ready to be put to death," and there is good reason to believe some of them actually faced execution. There is no evidence they ever waivered. Their convictions were not based on secondhand testimony, but their own personal experience with the risen Christ. They truly believed Jesus was the risen Messiah, and they banked their lives on it.

It is difficult to imagine what more a group of ancient witnesses could have done to show greater depth of sincerity and commitment to the truth.[32]

Despite the claims of skeptics, the evidence of history is on Christianity's side.

Question 22

Do the majority of Christians believe that you can't be a good person without being a Christian?[33]

It's just the opposite.

I'm a Christian because I know I'm a horrible person and the only hope I have is Jesus.

Question 23

Why do the Gospels differ in Jesus' response to the High Priest when asked if he is the Messiah? He either answers cryptically or in the affirmative.[34]

This is one of the most fascinating questions about Jesus' last week alive.

Many people charge the Gospels with contradiction, seeing how they record different trials and different responses. But there is no contradiction.

The trials of Jesus are one of the key places demonstrating that **when you combine all four Gospels into one account, they harmonize beautifully.**

It's one of the greatest signs of divine authorship in the Gospels. On their own, each makes perfect sense and possesses a unique style. But when you combine them, they form one coherent, seamless narrative. Such individuality yet perfect harmony would be difficult enough for modern-day writers, let alone four separate writers composing from different countries and decades. There is a Divine hand at work in these words.

The original question asks, *"Why do the Gospels differ in Jesus' response to the High Priest when asked if he is the Messiah? He either answers cryptically or in the affirmative."*

The answer is:

Jesus endured six trials before the Crucifixion. He answers cryptically or clearly depending on whom He is speaking to.

No single Gospel records all six. Each writer records the ones that match their focus. Also, each Gospel relies on eye-witness testimony; Mark, for example, records the eye-witness testimony of Peter. Thus, Mark focuses more on Peter's denials of Jesus rather than on Jesus' trials. Luke, on the other hand, interviewed multiple eye-witnesses and includes detailed accounts of multiple trials.

The trials are:

Jewish Ecclesiastical Trials

1:00 am — **1.** Preliminary hearing before Annas (John 18:12–13). *A trial before dawn was illegal in Jewish law. Annas uses the opportunity to find out who Jesus' disciples were, perhaps to find out who else they need to arrest.*

3:00 am — **2.** Before high priest and Sanhedrin (Mark 14:53; John 18:24). *This trial is also an illegal night trial. They use this opportunity to throw as many charges at Jesus as possible, in order to find a charge that will stick. Once they have this, they can take Jesus to the Romans.*

6:00 am — **3.** Before high priest and whole Sanhedrin (Jewish Supreme Court) (Luke 22:66). *This trial is barely legal, taking place after the first blush of sunrise. They assemble the full Sanhedrin to make their findings during the night official, according to Jewish law.*

Roman Civil Trials

7:00 am — **4.** Before Pilate (John 18:28). *Pilate finds Jesus innocent, but the religious authorities will not be assuaged. Pilate sends Jesus to Herod, hoping that Herod will deal with the problem.*

8:00 am — **5.** Before Herod Antipas, Ruler of Galilee (Luke 23:6). *Herod wants to see Jesus perform miracles like magic tricks. When He won't, Herod sends him back to Pilate.*

9:00 am — **6.** Before Pilate again (only the Romans could give the Jews the authority to execute a prisoner) (Luke 23:11). *Pilate again finds Jesus innocent, but to avoid a riot, he condemns Jesus to death with Jesus' permission.*

It's one thing to hear about the four Gospels combining seamlessly. It's another thing to see it yourself.

To demonstrate this incredible harmony, I'll copy the text of *Jesus Christ, the Greatest Life*, which combines all four Gospels into one smooth account. It uses all the words of the four Gospels, adds nothing, and leaves nothing out.

If you want to check the validity of the work yourself, I'll include all the verse references. You can double-check that every detail from every verse is included.

The story is fascinating. This drama has captivated the world for 2,000 years. When you read the full account together, it's easy to see why:

Jesus' First Trial: Preliminary Hearing before Annas, Former High Priest

Matt. 26:57, Mark 14:53, Luke 22:54a, John 18:12–14, 19–24

> Then the cohort of soldiers and the chief captain and the officers of the Jews took and bound Jesus.
>
> They led Him away first to Annas because he was the father-in-law of Caiaphas, who was the high priest that year. (It was Caiaphas who had advised the Jews that it would be prudent for one man to die for the people.)
>
> The high priest questioned Jesus about His disciples and His teaching. Jesus answered him, "I spoke openly to the world. I always taught in the synagogues and in the temple where all the Jews assemble. I said nothing in secret. Why do you question Me? Question those who heard Me. They know what I said."

When He said this, one of the officers standing nearby struck Jesus in the face. "Is this the way You answer the high priest?" he demanded.

"If I spoke wrongly," Jesus answered, "explain my error. But if I have spoken rightly, why do you strike Me?"

Jesus' Second Trial: Hearing Before Caiaphas

Matt. 26:59–68, Mark 14:55–65, Luke 22:63–65

Then Annas sent Him, still bound, to Caiaphas the high priest. Those who had seized Jesus led Him away to the high priest's house, where all the chief priests and the elders and teachers of the law had gathered.

The chief priests and the elders and the entire Sanhedrin kept trying to find false witnesses to testify against Jesus in order to execute Him. They could find none. Though many false witnesses came forward to accuse Him, their testimony did not agree.

At last two stepped forward and spoke against Him: "We heard this Man say, 'I'll destroy this 1temple of God made by human hands, and in three days I'll build another, not made by human hands.' " But even then their statements did not agree.

So the high priest stood up before them and questioned Jesus. "Do You refuse to answer?" he demanded. "What is this they're accusing You of?"

But Jesus was silent and made no answer.

Once more the high priest said to Him, "Are You the Messiah, the Son of the Blessed One? I charge You under oath by the living God: tell us whether You're the Messiah, the Son of God."

"It's just as you have said," Jesus answered. "I AM. Furthermore, I tell all of you that later on you will see the Son of Man sitting by the right hand of power and coming on the clouds of heaven."

Then the high priest tore his clothes and said, "He has spoken blasphemy! Why do we need any more witnesses? Listen, you have heard His blasphemy. What do you think?"

"He deserves to die!" they answered. Everyone condemned Him as deserving death.

Some of them began to spit in His face and strike Him with their fists. The men who were holding Jesus began to mock Him. After they had blindfolded Him, they kept slapping His face and taunting Him. "Prophesy!" they said. "Prophesy to us, You 'Messiah'! Who just struck You?"

And they said many other insulting things to Him.

Jesus' Third Trial: Before the Sanhedrin

Matt. 27:1–2, Mark 15:1, Luke 22:66–23:1

> As soon as daylight came, all the elders of the people—both the chief priests and the teachers of the law—met together against Jesus to execute Him. They brought Him up to the whole Sanhedrin and said, "If You are the Messiah, tell us."
>
> He said to them, "If I were to tell you, you would certainly not believe. And if I were to ask the questions, you would not answer Me or let Me go. But from now on the Son of Man will be seated by the right hand of the power of God!"
>
> "So You are the Son of God?" they all said.
>
> "It's just as you say," He replied, "because I AM."
>
> "Why do we need further witnesses?" they said. "We have heard it ourselves from His own mouth!"
>
> Then the whole crowd arose and tied up Jesus and took Him to appear before Pontius Pilate, the governor.

Jesus' Fourth Trial: First Hearing Before Pilate

Matt. 27:11–14, Mark 15:2–5, Luke 23:2–3, John 18:28–38a

Then the Jews led Jesus from Caiaphas to the Roman judgment hall, where Jesus stood before the governor. Because it was early, they did not go into the judgment hall. (They didn't want to become defiled and be unable to eat the Passover.)

So Pilate went out to them. "Of what are you accusing this Man?" he asked them.

"If He were not a criminal," they answered, "we wouldn't have brought Him to you."

"Take Him and judge Him according to your law," Pilate replied.

"We aren't permitted to execute anyone," the Jews responded. (In this way they were fulfilling what Jesus said about the kind of death He would suffer.)

They began accusing Him, saying, "We found this man subverting our nation and forbidding us to give tribute to Caesar. He says He's the Messiah, a king."

The chief priests and elders continued making many accusations against Jesus. But He made no reply.

"Do You refuse to answer?" Pilate said. "Don't You hear how many accusations they're charging You with?"

Jesus remained silent, 1not answering a single charge. The governor was astonished.

Pilate then went back to the judgment hall and called Jesus. "Are You the King of the Jews?" he asked Him.

Jesus replied, "It's just as you say. Are you asking this on your own, or did others tell you about Me?"

"Am I a Jew?" Pilate answered. "Your own nation and the chief priests handed You over to me. What have You done?"

Jesus said, "My kingdom is not of this world. If My kingdom were of this world, My servants would fight to keep Me from being handed over to the Jews. But at present My kingdom is not from here."

"Then You really are a king?" Pilate said.

Jesus answered, "It's just as you say. I am a king—I was born for this, and for this I came into the world, so I might testify to the truth. Everyone who belongs to the truth hears My voice."

"What is truth?" Pilate asked.

Jesus' Fifth Trial: Hearing Before Herod Antipas

Luke 23:4–12, John 18:38b

After saying this, Pilate went out again to the Jews and said to the chief priests and the crowds, "I find this Man guilty of nothing."

But they strongly insisted, "He is stirring up the people. He is teaching throughout Judea, starting from Galilee and reaching even to this place."

When Pilate heard this, he asked whether the Man was a Galilean. On learning that He was from the jurisdiction of Herod, he sent Him up to Herod, who happened to be in Jerusalem at the time.

When Herod saw Jesus, he was quite pleased. For a long time he had wanted to see Him since he had heard many reports about Him and hoped to see Him perform some miracle. He probed Him with many questions. But Jesus didn't answer them even though the priests and teachers of the law stood there viciously accusing Him.

After Herod and his soldiers had ridiculed and mocked Him, they clothed Him in a gaudy robe and sent Him back to Pilate. From that day on Pilate and Herod became friends; before this they did not get along.

Jesus' Sixth Trial: Final Hearing Before Pilate

Matt. 27:15–31, Mark 15:6–20, Luke 23:13–25, John 18:39–19:16

Then Pilate called together the chief priests and the rulers of the people and said to them, "You brought this Man to me on the charge of stirring up subversion. Yet on examining Him I found no substance to your accusations. Neither did Herod because he sent Him back to us. You can see He's done nothing deserving death.

"Now, you have a custom directing me to release one man to you at Passover. So I'll punish Him and then release Him." (At the feast the governor's custom was to release one prisoner to the people, whomever they chose. At that time a notable prisoner named Barabbas was being held along with a few of his fellow insurgents. He was a robber who had been thrown into prison for an insurrection in the city and for murder.)

When the crowds had gathered and noisily asked Pilate to act on the custom, he answered, "Whom do you want me to release to you? Barabbas, or Jesus, who is called 'Messiah'?" (He knew the chief priests had handed Jesus over because of envy. And as he was sitting on the judgment seat, his wife sent word to him: "Don't do anything to that just Man! On account of Him I have suffered many things today in a dream!")

But the chief priests and the elders stirred up the crowds to ask Pilate to release Barabbas to them instead, and to execute Jesus.

"Which of the two do you want me to release to you?" the governor said. "Do you want me to release to you the King of the Jews?"

135

They replied, "Barabbas!" They all shouted together, "Not this Man! Get rid of Him, and give us Barabbas!"

Because Pilate wanted to release Jesus, he said to them once more, "Then what should I do with Jesus who is called 'Messiah,' whom you call 'King of the Jews'?"

Again they all shouted, "Let Him be crucified!" They continued crying out, "Crucify! Crucify Him!"

For the third time Pilate said to them, "Why, what evil has He done? I don't find that He's done anything deserving death. So after punishing Him, I'll release Him."

Pilate took Jesus and had Him flogged. The soldiers took thorns, wove them into a crown, and placed it on His head. They put a purple garment on Him and said, "Hail, King of the Jews!" and kept punching Him with their fists.

Pilate then came out again and said to them, "Look, I am bringing Him out to you so you'll know I find Him not guilty." Jesus came out, wearing the crown of thorns and the purple garment. "Look at the Man!" Pilate said to them.

When the chief priests and the officers saw Him, they shouted, "Crucify! Crucify!"

"You take Him and crucify Him yourself," Pilate said. "I find Him not guilty."

"We have a law," the Jews answered, "and by our law He ought to die because He claimed to be the Son of God."

When Pilate heard this claim, he grew even more afraid. He returned to the judgment hall and said to Jesus, "Where do You come from?"

Jesus gave no answer.

"You refuse to talk to me?" Pilate said. "Don't You know I have authority to crucify You—or to release You?"

Jesus answered, "You would have no authority at all over Me unless it had been given to you from above. Because of this the one who handed Me over to you is guilty of the greater sin."

These words prompted Pilate to continue seeking ways to release Him. But the Jews shouted, "If you release this Man, you're no friend of Caesar. Anyone claiming to be the king is speaking against Caesar!"

Hearing this, Pilate brought Jesus outside. He sat down on the judgment seat in a place called the Pavement (or in the Jewish language, "Gabbatha"). It was Preparation Day for the Passover, about six in the morning. He said to the Jews, "Look at your king."

But they shouted, "Away with Him! Away with Him! Crucify Him!" They were insistent and shouted all the more, demanding loudly that He be crucified.

Pilate said to them, "Should I crucify your king?"

"We have no king," the chief priests answered, "except Caesar!"

When Pilate saw he couldn't dissuade them, but instead a riot was in the making, he took water and washed his hands in front of the crowd and said, "I am innocent of the blood of this righteous Man. You will be witnesses of the fact."

All the people answered, "His blood be on us and on our children!"

Their voices and those of the chief priests won out. So Pilate, wanting to satisfy the crowd, ordered that they should get what they demanded. He released Barabbas to them—the man they had asked for, who had been thrown into prison for insurrection and murder—but he gave in to their demands about Jesus and handed Him over to be crucified.

Then the governor's soldiers took Jesus and led Him away to the court called the Praetorium.

There they gathered the whole company of soldiers around Him. They stripped Him, then again clothed Him in purple, and put a crimson cloak on Him. And they put on His head the crown of thorns they had made, and placed a reed in His right hand. They continued mocking Him, 1bowing in homage and saying "Hail, 'King' of the Jews!" They spat on Him and took the reed from Him and kept beating Him on His head.

When they finished ridiculing Him, the soldiers stripped Him of the cloak and the purple garments and gave Him His own clothing. Then they led Him out to crucify Him.[35]

Question 24

Do you agree with Sarah Sanders' belief that God wanted Trump to be president? Why do you think this is so?[36]

According to what God said about this: **God appoints every President, King, Queen, Prime Minister, and Dictator, in every country around the world.**

That would mean that, yes, God wanted Trump to be President.

It also means that God wanted Obama to be President, George W. Bush to be President, and yes, even Bill Clinton to be President. God picked each one of them for the job.

And whoever we will have for our next President — whichever party, ethnicity, gender, or ideology — God picked that person to be President, as well.

God couldn't be clearer:

> Let every person be subject to the governing authorities. **For there is no authority except from God, and those that exist have been instituted by God.** (Romans 13:1–2 ESV)

Based on this, we can look at any ruler in power in any country. The simple fact that they are in power means that God wanted them to have that power.

But don't miss this: **just because God picked them does not mean that God endorses what they do.**

God holds leaders to account just as He does everyone else. The Bible is full of accounts of God judging the kings and queens of Israel and Judah. Even a man like King David, whom God calls a man after His own heart, cannot escape God's judgment for his own sins.

But God will raise up particular leaders for particular purposes.

For example, when God sought to deliver Israel from Egypt, He had this to say to the Pharaoh who clashed with Moses:

> But for this purpose **I have raised you up**, to show you my power, so that my name may be proclaimed in all the earth. (Exodus 9:16 ESV)

God certainly did not condone the Pharaoh's actions. But God used them to contrast His power to that of Pharaoh and his Egyptian gods. The God of Israel was able to rescue every single Israelite out of Egypt without losing a single Israelite life, while looting a great deal of gold and silver. Meanwhile, the Egyptian gods could do nothing to stop it.

In this case, God picked that particular Pharaoh to rule over Egypt at that particular time — not because God affirmed everything that Pharaoh chose to do, but so that God could glorify Himself in comparison to the powerless Egyptian deities.

To get back to the question:

Do you agree with Sarah Sanders' belief that God wanted Trump to be president?

Yes — if you agree that God also wanted Obama to be President.

But if she was saying that Trump was unique, that God wanted him to be President but God didn't want Obama to be President, then no, I disagree with that. So does the Bible.

Why do you think this is so?

God has specific things in mind for Trump to do, just as He had specific things in mind for Obama to do.

God considers the President — and every political ruler, at every level of government — to be His servant. He says so repeatedly:

> For rulers are not a terror to good conduct, but to bad. Would you have no fear of the one who is in authority? Then do what is good, and you will receive his approval, for **he is God's servant** for your good. But if you do wrong, be afraid, for he does not bear the sword in vain. For **he is the**

servant of God, an avenger who **carries out God's wrath** on the wrongdoer.

Therefore one must be in subjection, not only to avoid God's wrath but also for the sake of conscience. For because of this you also pay taxes, for **the authorities are ministers of God**, attending to this very thing. Pay to all what is owed to them: taxes to whom taxes are owed, revenue to whom revenue is owed, respect to whom respect is owed, honor to whom honor is owed. (Romans 13:3–7 ESV)

This might be shocking to read today. Obama was God's servant? Trump is God's servant? An atheistic mayor is God's servant? A gay congressperson is God's servant?

Yes, in all four cases.

The logic is clear: rulers generally try to protect their people. No one makes a law that you must drive at least 90 mph with your seatbelt unbuckled. Instead, they say you must drive at a safe speed, with your seatbelt buckled, and carry insurance in case of accidents. Generally, governments try to keep their people safe.

Yet even when the government is evil, God still requires us to honor them.

This doesn't mean we have to obey evil commands or submit ourselves to death. In the early days of Israel, King Saul tried to murder David repeatedly in cold blood.

To be clear: Saul's intent was evil. He wanted to murder David simply because God had picked David to be the next king of Israel.

Yet David would not dishonor Saul. Twice David had the chance to kill him. His men encouraged him to do so; no one would have blamed David for killing the man who had unleashed armies against him!

But David would not lay a hand against Saul, because God had anointed him to rule Israel. Even though Saul was acting foolishly and wickedly, David honored the leadership position God had given to him. Listen to the way David honors Saul, even as he resists the evil intent of Saul's heart:

> Then David shouted to Saul, "Why do you listen to the people who say I am trying to harm you? This very day you can see with your own eyes it isn't true. For the Lord placed you at my mercy back there in the cave. Some of my men told me to kill you, but I spared you. For I said, '**I will never harm the king—he is the Lord's anointed one.**' Look, my father, at what I have in my hand. It is a piece of the hem of your robe! I cut it off, but I didn't kill you. This proves that I am not trying to harm you and that I have not sinned against you, even though you have been hunting for me to kill me.
>
> "May the Lord judge between us. Perhaps the Lord will punish you for what you are trying to do to

me, **but I will never harm you.**" (1 Samuel 24:9–12 NLT)

Did God want Saul to be King? Yes, God picked Saul specifically.

Did God want Saul to murder David? No, but God used Saul's wickedness to highlight David's purity of heart, demonstrating to all how qualified David was to rule.

Does God want Trump to be President? Yes. After Trump, God might pick a Democrat to be President. Then God might throw us all for a loop and pick an Independent to follow up. Each will be God's servant.

And for each one, God will have specific purposes in mind for that ruler to accomplish that only that particular person can do.

Question 25

Do Christians mind being friends with people who hate everything about Christianity?[37]

We enjoy it, actually.

Some of my best friends through life don't agree with my theological views. The strange thing is that you can actually have a really good time playing Settlers of Catan and watching *Lord of the Rings* together even when you don't agree on everything.

Some of my friends have become Christians. Some haven't. Yet we're still friends. That's how friendship works.

But to be completely fair to the question, none of my friends *hate* everything about Christianity. They may disagree, even disagree passionately, but I don't believe any of them *hate* Christianity.

I haven't encountered many people who truly hate Christianity. I've chatted with a few people online, including several here on Quora, who are antagonistic to Christianity, but that doesn't stop me from trying to be friendly towards them. Arguments can get heated, but that's no reason not to honor the other person or listen respectfully to all they have to say. I'm certainly not perfect in being kind to everyone, but I'm trying to improve as time goes on.

I've found that when people hate you, the best thing to do is love them back.

It's what the founder of Christianity taught:

> "You have heard the law that says, 'Love your neighbor' and hate your enemy. But I say, *love your enemies!*" (Matthew 5:43–44 NLT).

Question 26

What would Jesus say about Christianity today?[38]

Well, which Christians are you talking about?

There are 2 to 3 billion Christians around the world today. They don't all look alike.

You have major groups, like the Catholics, Protestants, and Orthodox; you have minor groups like the Baptists, Presbyterians, Methodists, Anglicans, and Lutherans; you have local groups like individual churches and home groups.

Among these, some are doing really well. They look a lot like Jesus.

Others are doing horribly. They look a lot like Jesus' enemies.

Still others are growing, looking a bit more like Jesus every day, but they acknowledge they have a long, long way to go, yet.

It has always been this way. Be very careful of saying "All Christians are like this," or "Jesus would be disappointed with Christians today." Christians are far too diverse to label so wantonly.

Hope You're Curious

If you read Revelation 2–3, you'll find Jesus talking specifically to seven local churches. Some He praises. Others He warns.

One church in particular, Laodicea, struggles with many of the same things western, American churches face: the temptation of money, focusing on material possessions, using Jesus to get stuff, and living out their own personal desires with little concern for what God desires.

To this church, Jesus says:

> I know you inside and out, and find little to my liking. You're not cold, you're not hot—far better to be either cold or hot! You're stale. You're stagnant. You make me want to vomit. You brag, 'I'm rich, I've got it made, I need nothing from anyone,' oblivious that in fact you're a pitiful, blind beggar, threadbare and homeless.
>
> Here's what I want you to do: Buy your gold from me, gold that's been through the refiner's fire. Then you'll be rich. Buy your clothes from me, clothes designed in Heaven. You've gone around half-naked long enough. And buy medicine for your eyes from me so you can see, *really* see.
>
> The people I love, I call to account—prod and correct and guide so that they'll live at their best. Up on your feet, then! About face! Run after God!
>
> Look at me. I stand at the door. I knock. If you hear me call and open the door, I'll come right in and sit

down to supper with you. Conquerors will sit alongside me at the head table, just as I, having conquered, took the place of honor at the side of my Father. That's my gift to the conquerors!

Are your ears awake? Listen. Listen to the Wind Words, the Spirit blowing through the churches. (Revelation 3:15–22, The Message).

At the other end of the spectrum, consider this church:

The Golden Lampstand Church in Shanxi Province was destroyed this week by paramilitary police officers, according to local news reports and foreign activists. Credit: ChinaAid, via Associated Press.

To them, Jesus would say something similar to what He said to the ancient church in Smyrna:

I can see your pain and poverty—constant pain, dire poverty—but I also see your wealth. And I hear the lie in the claims of those who pretend to be good Jews, who in fact belong to Satan's crowd.

Fear nothing in the things you're about to suffer—but stay on guard! Fear nothing! The Devil is about to throw you in jail for a time of testing—ten days. It won't last forever.

Don't quit, even if it costs you your life. Stay there believing. I have a Life-Crown sized and ready for you.

Are your ears awake? Listen. Listen to the Wind Words, the Spirit blowing through the churches. Christ-conquerors are safe from Devil-death. (Revelation 2:9–11, The Message).

What would Jesus say to Christians today? The same things He said to Christians in Revelation 2–3. It turns out we're still struggling with the same things.

Question 27

What are some of the best ways to express "I love you" without actually saying it?[39]

Sacrifice.

Selfishness is innate in human beings. We begin selfish as babies, concerned only with our own immediate needs. As we grow, we learn that other people exist and have needs, as well. But that innate desire to gratify yourself before anyone else still rages powerfully inside each of us.

But what happens when you love someone?

You put them before you.

As the saying goes, "Greater love has no one than this: laying down your life for your friends."

We all agree that a friend who sacrifices their life to save yours truly loved you. But this isn't limited to the extreme situations. Even in the almost-unnoticeable daily sacrifices, laying down your life proves your love:

- When you're watching TV but a chore needs to be done, you get up and do the chore so that your loved one doesn't have to.

- When the baby cries at night, you get up to take care of it, so your loved one can sleep.

- When you're picking a place to eat, you cheerfully set aside your preference and choose theirs.

- When you get home and the place is messy, you don't leave it for them to deal with. You start cleaning immediately, so that when they arrive home they can relax.

- When you're both exhausted but you need to drive home, you volunteer to drive so they can sleep on the way.

This applies to far more than romance!

- If you ever wonder whether your mom or dad loves you, consider all the sacrifices they willingly make to put your needs ahead of theirs.

- If you ever wonder whether your boss loves you, look for sacrifice. Look for any way in which they sacrifice their desires to care for their employees. If they happily sacrifice to help you, you've found a great place to work.

- If you ever wonder whether you can trust a politician, look for their sacrifice. Don't listen to their words; anyone can say anything. Look for their sacrifice. Do they take as much as they can get for themselves? Or do they turn around and give as much as they can to help others, at the cost of denying themselves what they could have had?

- If you ever wonder whether a gift was truly heartfelt, consider the amount of sacrifice it took to give it to you. Did they invest the time necessary to make sure the gift was something you wanted or needed? Did they spend the minimum amount of time on it or did they make sure it communicated that they care?

Love is demonstrated by sacrifice.

I don't think love can exist without it. Have you ever encountered someone who truly loves you but won't sacrifice for you? I haven't, either.

You know someone loves you when they willingly sacrifice for you.

And the flip side:

You can say "I love you" simply by sacrificing for the person you cherish.

The more you sacrifice, the more powerful the statement is.

But what happens if you always sacrifice? Won't your partner abuse your trust and keep making you sacrifice everything you care about?

Not if they love you. If they love you, they'll be sacrificing right back. And there are few relationships more beautiful than when both people are eager to sacrifice to make their loved one happy.

To close, let me quote the immortal words of a 5-year old:

"Love is when you give someone else the last chicken nugget."

Question 28

Is Jesus Christ the Son of God or God?[40]

He is both. **Jesus is the Son of God and Jesus is God.**

Many Christians are subtly frustrated with Jesus over this. Why does Jesus keep using titles like "Son of God" and "Son of Man?" Why can't Jesus just say "I am God?"

He did. But He said it in a way that 1st century Jewish ears would understand.

Consider Matthew 3:17:

And a voice from heaven said, "**This is my Son**, whom I love; with him I am well pleased."

This is Jesus' introduction to the world. God could have used any possible descriptor of Jesus at this point. So why on earth does God the Father start by saying that Jesus is His Son?

To modern, Western ears, being called "son" doesn't mean much. We assume it means any male child. To our ears, every boy who exists is the son of his father.

But to a first-century Jewish ear, the word "son" was a precise technical term. You would never call someone a "son" until they had earned the title.

If you could travel back to Israel in the time of Jesus and you asked a man on the street whether he had any sons, he might say to you, "Yes! I'm proud to say that I have three boys and one son." By saying this, he is not declaring favoritism for one child over the others. Rather, he is rejoicing in the fact that one of his boys has finally become his son.

As every male child began his life as a baby, he was considered a boy. He would enjoy his boyhood playing with his siblings and friends, as most children do.

Yet there would come a point at which this young boy would be ready to leave his childhood behind and become a man. This would typically happen around the age of 12, 13, or 14, depending on the child. They would hold a ceremony called the *bar-mitzvah*, which celebrated this young boy becoming a young man. He would now begin his life's work, often apprenticing to his father and learning the family trade.

Once this boy had officially a man, he could finally be called the son of his father. **To call someone a son declared that this son was now the same as his father.**

A boy could not be called a son, because he was still a boy, playing games and amusing himself with toys, while his father was an adult man who was busy about his life's work. But as soon as that boy himself became an adult man, setting aside boyhood diversions in favor of his life's work, he could now be called a son, because he and his father were the same.

This carried over into common Jewish expressions. To identify a person with a certain characteristic or fate, it was common to say they were the son of that quality. For example, in John 17:12, Jesus refers to Judas as "the son of destruction," as Judas carries out his plot of betrayal against Jesus. By this, Jesus was not saying anything about Judas' parents. Rather, He was stating that Judas' crime was so severe that he would unavoidably be destroyed because of it. Judas had sealed his own fate by betraying innocent blood, so much so that Jesus could describe Judas as becoming one with destruction. To be a son meant that you were one with your father. To be the son of destruction meant that Judas was one with destruction.

Therefore, when God the Father declares Jesus to be His Son, He is declaring clearly and unequivocally that Jesus is the same as His Father.

They are one; they are both God. Or to say it more precisely, Jesus is the same God who has been worshiped throughout the entire Old Testament, and He has now taken on flesh to live among and redeem His people.

This claim was unmistakable to the Jewish ear. When Jesus was arrested and placed on trial, the chief priests sought in vain for witnesses who could accuse Jesus of any wrongdoing. Yet they had no need of them. When they asked Jesus plainly, **"Are you the Son of God, then?"** Jesus responded, **"You say rightly. I am."** They exploded with fury, declaring, "What further testimony do we need? We have heard it ourselves from his own lips!" (Luke 22:70-71).

They held no doubt about who Jesus said He was. **By stating that He was the Son of God, Jesus declared Himself to be equal with God**, to be the same as His Father in Heaven. The Gospel of John makes it absolutely explicit, declaring:

> "This was why the Jews were seeking all the more to kill him, because not only was he breaking the Sabbath, but **he was even calling God his own Father, making himself equal with God**" (John 5:18 ESV)

The chief priests heard these words as blasphemy. Don't miss this!

If being the Son of God meant anything other than claiming to be God, **it would not have been blasphemy.** Blasphemy means to speak words about God that are untrue.

If "Son of God" meant that Jesus was spiritual, or a gifted spiritual leader, or a messenger from God, or anything else other than claiming to be God, it would have been a mere disagreement. The chief priests might not have liked it or agreed with it, but it wouldn't have blasphemy.

Both Jesus' followers and Jesus' enemies realized that **to be the Son of God is to be God.**

That's how the Jewish language worked in the 1st century. Jesus could not have claimed to be God any clearer than to say that He is the only Son of God.

So is Jesus the Son of God? Yes.

Is Jesus God? Yes.

The two phrases mean the same thing.

Question 29

What evidence is there for Jesus Christ's death, burial, and resurrection?[41]

This is one of the most important questions you will ever ask.

If Jesus Christ died, was buried, and rose again, then it changes everything. It means that death is defeated. It means that Jesus can do things no mere human could ever do. It means that what Jesus said about Himself is true — that He is God come in the flesh.

But if Jesus did not rise from death, then we can confidently forget about Him and everything He said.

What, then, is the evidence? Why should we believe something so outrageous as the idea that a human being didn't stay dead?

It turns out that the evidence is staggering.

We could take this conversation in several directions. But to find the widest possible appeal, we will focus on evidence that virtually every scholar agrees with: conservative and liberal, religious and skeptical, ancient and modern.

What, then, do virtually all scholars agree on?

Let's break this into two pieces: Jesus' death and Jesus' Resurrection:

> *Jesus's Trial and Crucifixion.*
>
> According to the gospels Jesus was condemned by the Jewish high court on the charge of blasphemy and then delivered to the Romans for execution for the treasonous act of setting himself up as King of the Jews. Not only are these facts confirmed by independent biblical sources like Paul and the Acts of the Apostles, but they are also confirmed by extra-biblical sources. From Josephus and Tacitus, we learn that Jesus was crucified by Roman authority under the sentence of Pontius Pilate. From Josephus and Mara bar Serapion we learn that the Jewish leaders made a formal accusation against Jesus and participated in events leading up to his crucifixion. And from the Babylonian Talmud, Sanhedrin 43a, we learn that Jewish involvement in the trial was explained as a proper undertaking against a heretic. According to Johnson, **"The support for the mode of his death, its agents, and perhaps its coagents, is overwhelming: Jesus faced a trial before his death, was condemned and executed by crucifixion."** [11] The crucifixion of Jesus is recognized even by the Jesus Seminar as **"one indisputable fact."** [12]

But that raises the very puzzling question: Why was Jesus crucified? As we have seen, the evidence indicates that his crucifixion was instigated by his blasphemous claims, which to the Romans would come across as treasonous. That's why he was crucified, in the words of the plaque that was nailed to the cross above his head, as "The King of the Jews." But if Jesus was just a peasant, cynic philosopher, just a liberal social gadfly, as the Jesus Seminar claims, then his crucifixion becomes inexplicable. As Professor Leander Keck of Yale University has said, "The idea that this Jewish cynic (and his dozen hippies) with his demeanor and aphorisms was a serious threat to society sounds more like a conceit of alienated academics than sound historical judgement." [13] New Testament scholar John Meier is equally direct. He says that a bland Jesus who just went about spinning out parables and telling people to look at the lilies of the field-- "such a Jesus," he says, "would threaten no one, just as the university professors who create him threaten no one." [14] The Jesus Seminar has created Jesus who is incompatible with the one indisputable fact of his crucifixion.

[11] Luke Timothy Johnson, *The Real Jesus* (San Francisco: Harper San Francisco, 1996), p. 125.
[12] Robert Funk, Jesus Seminar videotape.
[13] Leander Keck, "The Second Coming of the Liberal Jesus?" *Christian Century* (August, 1994), p. 786.
[14] John P. Meier, *A Marginal Jew,* vol. 1: *The Roots of the Problem and the Person,* Anchor Bible Reference Library (New York: Doubleday, 1991), p. 177.[42]

Did you catch that?

Even the sharpest critics of the Bible agree that Jesus' death on a Roman cross is an indisputable historical fact.

But that's only part of the puzzle. Everybody dies. What about the Resurrection? **What can we learn about the Resurrection from the facts that virtually all scholars agree with?**

The resurrection of Jesus.

It seems to me that there are four established facts which constitute inductive evidence for the resurrection of Jesus:

Fact #1: *After his crucifixion, Jesus was buried by Joseph of Arimathea in the tomb.* This fact is highly significant because it means that the location of Jesus's tomb was known to Jew and Christian alike. In that case it becomes inexplicable how belief in his resurrection could arise and flourish in the face of a tomb containing his corpse. According to the late John A. T. Robinson of Cambridge University, the honorable burial of Jesus is one of "the earliest and best-attested facts about Jesus." [15]

Fact #2: *On the Sunday morning following the crucifixion, the tomb of Jesus was found empty by a group of his women followers.* According to Jakob Kremer, an Austrian specialist on the resurrection, "By far most exegetes hold firmly to the reliability of the biblical statements concerning the empty tomb." [16] As D. H. van Daalen points out, "It is extremely difficult to object to the empty tomb on historical grounds; those who deny it do so on the basis of theological or philosophical assumptions." [17]

Fact #3: *On multiple occasions and under various circumstances, different individuals and groups of people experienced appearances of Jesus alive from the dead.* This is a fact that is almost universally acknowledged among New Testament scholars today. Even Gert Lüdemann, perhaps the most prominent current critic of the resurrection, admits, "It may be taken as historically certain that Peter and the disciples had experiences after Jesus's death in which Jesus appeared to them as the risen Christ." [18]

Finally, fact #4: *The original disciples believed that Jesus was risen from the dead despite their having every reason not to.* Despite having every predisposition to the contrary, it is an undeniable fact of history that the original disciples believed in, proclaimed, and were willing to go to their deaths for the fact of Jesus's resurrection. C. F. D. Moule of Cambridge University concludes that we have here a belief which nothing in terms of prior historical influences can account for—apart from the resurrection itself. [19]

Any responsible historian, then, who seeks to give an account of the matter, must deal with these four independently established facts: the honorable burial of Jesus, the discovery of his empty tomb, his appearances alive after his death, and the very origin of the disciples' belief in his resurrection and, hence, of Christianity itself. **I want to emphasize that these four facts represent, not the conclusions of conservative scholars, nor have I quoted conservative scholars, but represent rather the majority view of New Testament scholarship today. The question is: how do you best explain these facts?**

Now this puts the skeptical critic in a somewhat desperate situation. For example, some time ago I had a debate with a professor at the University of California, Irvine, on the historicity of the resurrection of Jesus. He had written his doctoral dissertation on the subject and was thoroughly familiar with the evidence. He could not deny the facts of Jesus's honorable burial, his empty tomb, his post-mortem appearances, and the origin of the disciples' belief in his resurrection. Therefore, his only recourse was to come up with some alternative explanation of these facts. And so he argued that *Jesus had an unknown identical twin brother* who was separated from him at birth, came back to Jerusalem just at the time of the crucifixion, stole Jesus's body out of the grave, and presented himself to the disciples, who mistakenly inferred that Jesus was risen from the dead! Now I won't go into how I went about refuting his theory, but I think that this theory is instructive because **it shows to what desperate lengths skepticism must go in order to deny the historicity of the resurrection of Jesus. In fact, the evidence is so powerful that one of today's leading *Jewish* theologians Pinchas Lapide has declared himself convinced on the basis of the evidence that the God of Israel raised Jesus from the dead!** [20]

[15] John A. T. Robinson, *The Human Face of God* (Philadelphia: Westminster, 1973), p. 131.

[16] Jakob Kremer, *Die Osterevangelien--Geschichten um Geschichte* (Stuttgart: Katholisches Bibelwerk, 1977), pp. 49-50.

[17] D. H. Van Daalen, *The Real Resurrection* (London: Collins, 1972), p. 41.

[18] Gerd Lüdemann, *What Really Happened to Jesus?*, trans. John Bowden (Louisville, Kent.: Westminster John Knox Press, 1995), p. 80.

[19] C. F. D. Moule and Don Cupitt, "The Resurrection: a Disagreement," *Theology* 75 (1972): 507-19.

[20] Pinchas Lapide, *The Resurrection of Jesus*, trans. Wilhelm C. Linss (London: SPCK, 1983).[43]

There is other evidence we could consider — evidence from archaeology, from what additional ancient historians record, from the testimony of Jesus' enemies, from the lives and sacrifices of the Apostles, and on and on we could go.

But even if we limit ourselves only to the few facts that the most skeptical scholars agree with, we can still build

a tremendously powerful case that Jesus Christ died on a Roman cross and rose from death three days later.

This is why nearly a third of the world's population believes in Jesus Christ. The evidence is simply overwhelming.

Question 30

Does God kill people He hates by diseases and accidents?[44]

God's plan allowed Him to kill His own Son on the Cross. God the Father loves Jesus more than anything, yet in God's perfect plan, Jesus died.

God does not kill those He hates.

Jesus let Himself be killed in their place so that those who hate God can find love, peace, and joy in the God they used to reject.

Jesus loves so entirely that He asked God the Father to forgive the executioners who were murdering Him. He didn't want them to suffer for this crime. He wanted them forgiven so that their sin would not keep them away from God.

There has never been a love like God's!

Question 31

How would a skilled magician perform some of the alleged miracles of Jesus, only using the technology available at the time?[45]

They could not.

Jesus' miracles were not sleight-of-hand tricks. He didn't have a controlled space to manipulate or a limited selection of sick people, such that He could stage a fake healing.

From His first miracle to the last, Jesus worked **publicly**. His miracles were **verifiable** and **falsifiable**. That was the point of the miracles: to prove beyond doubt that Jesus had genuine supernatural powers.

Consider Jesus' first miracle, turning water into wine:

> Now there were **six stone water jars** there for the Jewish rites of purification, **each holding twenty or thirty gallons.** Jesus said to the servants, "Fill the jars with water." And they filled them up to the brim. And he said to them, "Now draw some out and take it to the master of the feast." So they took it.

> When the master of the feast tasted the water now become wine, and did not know where it came from (though the servants who had drawn the water knew), the master of the feast called the bridegroom and said to him, "Everyone serves the good wine first, and when people have drunk freely, then the poor wine. But you have kept the good wine until now."
>
> This, the first of his signs, Jesus did at Cana in Galilee, and manifested his glory. And his disciples believed in him. (John 2:6-11)

At a minimum, Jesus transformed 120 gallons of water into wine. This is no sleight-of-hand trick! There's no way to hide such a massive quantity of wine and slip it in while no one is looking. **That's why the disciples believed: they recognized no natural human power could have accomplished this.**

Notice the pattern: this was **public** (there was no bigger celebration than a wedding!), it was **verifiable** (the servants who filled the vessels with water could verify what they filled them with), and it was **falsifiable** (everyone could test the wine, check its quality, and check each of the storage vessels in turn).

Consider also Jesus' early healings:

> And immediately he left the synagogue and entered the house of Simon and Andrew, with James and

> John. Now Simon's mother-in-law lay ill with a fever, and immediately they told him about her. And he came and took her by the hand and lifted her up, and the fever left her, and she began to serve them.
>
> That evening at sundown **they brought to him all who were sick or oppressed by demons.** And **the whole city** was gathered together at the door. And **he healed many who were sick with various diseases, and cast out many demons**. And he would not permit the demons to speak, because they knew him. (Mark 1:29-34)

It's possible that Jesus could have staged the healing of Simon's mother-in-law, but to what point? It was a private scene with Jesus and a few disciples in a small house.

But word got out. And when it did, **every sick person in town** showed up to be healed. Again, there's no way to stage this. Everyone in town knew who was sick among them. If all of their sick people remained sick, but only a few mysterious visitors were "healed," they would have noticed! What amazed them all was watching Jesus completely heal people they knew who were legitimately sick.

Notice the pattern: this was **public** (the whole town showed up!), the healings were **verifiable** (everyone knew the people who were being healed), and if anyone came to ask about them in future years, they were **falsifiable**, because everyone in town was a witness. Further, Peter continued living in town, so if the healings turned out to be fake, guess who the townspeople would confront about it? But they didn't. Instead, word spread even further that Jesus could heal beyond the ability of any natural power.

Consider also Jesus' multiplying of food for thousands of people:

> When Jesus went ashore he saw a great crowd, and he had compassion on them and healed their sick.
>
> Now when it was evening, the disciples came to him and said, "This is a desolate place, and the day is now over; send the crowds away to go into the villages and buy food for themselves."
>
> But Jesus said, "They need not go away; you give them something to eat."
>
> They said to him, "We have only **five loaves here and two fish**."
>
> And he said, "Bring them here to me."
>
> Then he ordered the crowds to sit down on the grass, and taking the five loaves and the two fish, he looked up to heaven and said a blessing. Then he broke the loaves and gave them to the disciples, and the disciples gave them to the crowds. And they all ate and were satisfied. And they took up **twelve baskets full of the broken pieces left over**.

And those who ate were about **five thousand men, besides women and children**. (Matthew 14:14-21)

It's possible that Jesus and His disciples could have hidden a small amount of food in their robes or on their boat. But food for five thousand men, plus their wives and children? There's no way to smuggle such a vast quantity of food to a desolate place without notice.

Notice again the pattern: this was **public** (thousands of people witnessed the miracle and ate the food), it was **verifiable** (every single person held, smelled, tasted, and drew nourishment from the evidence of the miracle), and it was **falsifiable** (the leftovers were so numerous that even they couldn't have been smuggled in!).

Finally, consider how Jesus' enemies tried to smear Him:

> Then a demon-oppressed man who was **blind** and **mute** was brought to him, and he healed him, so that the man spoke and saw.
>
> And **all the people were amazed**, and said, "Can this be the Son of David?"
>
> But when the Pharisees heard it, they said, "It is only by Beelzebul, the prince of demons, that this man casts out demons." (Matthew 12:22-24)

These were the people who hated Jesus more than anyone else. They had every reason to destroy Jesus in any way possible.

And even they couldn't deny that Jesus worked genuine miracles! Their only explanation was to say that Jesus did them by the devil's power instead of by God's power. If anyone would have been searching for tricks or deceptions in Jesus' work, it was them. But they found none. All they found were genuine healings that they had to try to explain in some way so that people wouldn't believe that Jesus came from God.

So notice again the pattern: this healing was **public** (crowds witnessed it, even including Jesus' enemies), it was **verifiable** (even Jesus enemies agreed that a genuine miracle took place), and it was **falsifiable** (they wanted to deny it, but they couldn't, because the evidence of genuine healing was too strong).

Jesus' miracles couldn't be faked. He didn't allow them to be. The point of the miracles was to verify Jesus' identity.

This is why God gives people the ability to work miracles through the Bible: to verify their message and their status as divine messengers.

Anyone can claim to be the Son of God. But if Jesus claims to be God and then performs miracles that only God could perform for three and a half years, then His words have weight.

As the saying goes, extraordinary claims require extraordinary evidence. This is why Jesus gave three and a half years of extraordinary evidence: public, verifiable, falsifiable miracles that only the power of God could accomplish.

Question 32

Why are the Greek gods considered myths while the Christian God isn't?[46]

The Christian God is a myth.

But He's a myth that happens to be true.

Mythology serves a purpose: it provides answers to the questions of life. These include:

- Where did I come from?

- What am I doing here?

- Where am I going when I die?

- Where can I turn to for help when I'm in trouble?

- How do I know what's right and what's wrong?

Every human asks these questions. We can't escape them. Eventually people codify their answers into mythologies. These mythologies go by a variety of names: atheism, pantheism, Hinduism, Buddhism, Islam, Judaism, individualism, hedonism, elitism, nationalism, and of course, Christianity.

Every culture creates their own mythology because every culture has to answer these questions. A lot of times people come up with wrong answers. But sometimes they get the answers right.

To rephrase the question, then, we have this: **why did the Greek mythology die out while the Christianity mythology continues to grow?**

In answer this, many atheists (several who have written other answers to this question here on Quora) argue that Christianity will follow the Greek myths into oblivion. They argue that we are all atheists, because none of us believe in these Greek gods, nor in the plethora of other ancient deities. Surely the Christian God is just one more deity who will soon become irrelevant, like all these others.

This argument sounds persuasive until you scratch beneath the surface.

This argument uses its conclusion as its premise: that there are no actual deities. It is not an argument against the existence of God; it assumes that God doesn't exist and extrapolates from that assumption, without proving it.

But why is this kind of reasoning wrong?

Imagine a math class. The teacher writes a problem on the board. A dozen students all reach different answers as they work it out independently. At least 11 of these 12 answers will be wrong. But that doesn't mean that the 12th answer will inevitably be wrong, as well. It may indeed be the only correct answer. To find out, you have to evaluate the answer directly. Its truth or falsehood stands on its own merits, not the merits of others.

Why, then, has Christianity continued to grow when other mythologies, such as the ancient Greek mythology, have died out?

Because Christianity answers the questions of life better than any other mythology — including atheism.

Consider the way atheism attempts to answer the five questions listed above. (Please note that I'm not attempting to set up a straw man. This is an honest representation of how I've observed various atheists answer these questions in the past).

- Where did I come from? The atheist answers: *you came from a process that created the universe, which we still can't identify, but it was probably mindless. You came from a random series of mutations in various life forms over a long period of time. There was no purpose to your creation. You are a cosmic accident.*

- What am I doing here? The atheist answers: *You are trying to survive against every other form of life around you that's also trying to survive. The fittest, the best able to adapt, the most resourceful — these will survive. The rest will fail. Statistically speaking, you will probably fail.*

- Where am I going when I die? The atheist answers: *Nowhere. Death ends your existence. The universe doesn't care.*

- Where can I turn to for help when I'm in trouble? The atheist answers: *To yourself. There's no form of life higher than you that you can appeal to.*

- How do I know what's right and what's wrong? The atheist answers: *Ultimately there is no such thing as "right" and "wrong." Those are social constructs designed to promote the best chance for survival.*

Is it any wonder that so many atheists struggle with depression?

If that statement seems unfair, consider these findings from the *American Journal of Psychiatry:*

> **Religiously unaffiliated subjects had significantly more lifetime suicide attempts and more first-degree relatives who committed suicide** than subjects who endorsed a religious affiliation. Unaffiliated subjects were younger, less often married, less often had children, and had less contact with family members. Furthermore, **subjects with no religious affiliation perceived fewer reasons for living, particularly fewer moral objections to suicide.** In terms of clinical characteristics, religiously unaffiliated

subjects had more lifetime impulsivity, aggression, and past substance use.[47]

What you believe matters. It affects everything about your life.

This is why the Ancient Greek mythology died out: its answers to the big questions of life were just as unsatisfying.

- Where did I come from? The Ancient Greek answers: *You came from a pantheon of deities who either don't care about you personally or created you to be slaves.*

- What am I doing here? The Ancient Greek answers: *You are struggling to live out your life, just as the deities are. They fight and hate and love and struggle and kill, just as you do.*

- Where am I going when I die? The Ancient Greek answers: *To a meaningless afterlife. Souls flit around in Hades without a sense of purpose, wits, or strength to affect anything.*

- Where can I turn to for help when I'm in trouble? The Ancient Greek answers: *You can try to gain the attention of a deity through sacrifice and prayer, but there's no guarantee they'll hear or care enough to answer.*

- How do I know what's right and what's wrong? The Ancient Greek answers: *These debates are endless, because the gods themselves are just as petty, selfish, mean, and cruel as the worst humans. You should try to avoid "hubris," although there's a large debate about what it entails.*

This is ultimately why the Ancient Greek religion faded away. There were other factors, of course. But external factors are seldom as the answers the religion itself gives to life.

Compared to these, why has Christianity survived? More than that, why has Christianity grown so exponentially that there are more people on Earth who are Christians than people who are anything else?

Consider the way Christianity answers these questions:

- Where did I come from? The Christian answers: *You come from a loving, personal God who created you deliberately and designed you specifically to be exactly who you are. He made you this way because there are purposes and destinies for your life that only you can fulfill.*

- What am I doing here? The Christian answers: *You are living to enjoy God and the life He has created for you to enjoy. He designed this world as a place for you to delight in and steward well. He invites you to get to know Him — the source of all wisdom, all knowledge, all beauty, all satisfaction, all pleasure, all peace, all joy, and all love. He wants you to be full of all of these things.*

- Where am I going when I die? The Christian answers: *That depends on your choice. If you choose to follow this God, you go to be with Him — and you get to enjoy all that He is: wisdom, knowledge, beauty, satisfaction, pleasure, peace, joy, love. If you choose to reject this God, you reject all that He provides, and go to a place devoid of them. He won't force Himself on you. You get to choose which you prefer.*

- Where can I turn to for help when I'm in trouble? The Christian answers: *The same God who created the universe knows you and cares about you. He asks you to "cast yours cares upon Him, because He cares for you." More than that, He will use His power to help you.*

- How do I know what's right and what's wrong? The Christian answers: *Ultimately, to be good, you be like God: He sacrifices Himself for you because He loves you; He forgives you of anything if you ask; He will never stop loving you, no matter what you do or become; He will always welcome you into His presence if you choose to come; He will always have time for you; He will listen to everything you have to say; He will cherish His time with you; He will rejoice over you and all the uniqueness that you possess; He will always keep His word; He will*

183

never deceive you; He will provide for you. If you be like God, you'll be in good territory.

Can you see why Christianity thrives?

Of course, any good mythology not only provides good answers. It must also be objectively true.

For this, I ask you to consult the other answers in this book. The evidence for Christianity is astoundingly plentiful — in archaeology, in philosophy, in scientific discovery, in personal experience, and in virtually every other arena.

But these five questions reveal one of the primary ways we experience the truth of Christianity: **its coherence**.

When Christianity answers the big questions of life (and the smaller ones), it all makes sense as part of a whole. This is because it coalesces in one Person, the God who is unquestionably *good*.

But the biggest piece is this: this God is not merely someone you can read about. **You can experience Him. You can know Him. And you can find out that His promises come true.**

This is why Christianity is thriving today.

Question 33

Do you ever speculate about the details of Jesus' childhood?[48]

We don't have to speculate. The Bible tells us a great deal about Jesus' childhood, both directly and indirectly.

The key theme: **Jesus' childhood was normal.**

Granted, He probably upset the curve in school and never rebelled against His parents, but He did it in an ordinary fashion.

Or to say it clearly: **no one who observed Jesus' childhood concluded He was Messiah or God.** They thought He was a normal kid. A smart and obedient normal kid, but still normal.

How do we know?

Because the Bible records the reaction of all the people whom Jesus grew up around when He told them He was Messiah. And no one said "Of course! We always knew it!"

Instead, they were shocked and surprised:

> Everyone spoke well of him and was amazed by the gracious words that came from his lips. *"How can*

this be?" they asked. "Isn't this Joseph's son?" (Luke 4:22, NLT)

In other words, "How can this boy claim to be Messiah? Didn't he grow up down the street?"

Jesus was so *normal* as a child that those who grew up around Him found it hard to believe He would become anyone special.

From this, we can conclude several things:

- Jesus performed no miracles as a child.

- Jesus did not talk about being Messiah or claim to be God as a child.

- Jesus apprenticed to Joseph in the family trade of carpentry/stone masonry. This is what every normal child did — apprenticing to their parents.

- As an adult, before beginning His messianic work around age 30, Jesus worked a normal man's job.

Some people imagine Jesus testing His supernatural powers as a boy, such as shaping clay into a bird and breathing on it to give it life. But if Jesus had lived such a comic-book boyhood, no one would have been surprised to hear Him claim extraordinary things about Himself.

If Jesus was a normal boy, what else was He?

Smart.

> Now his parents went to Jerusalem every year at the Feast of the Passover.
>
> And when he was **twelve years old**, they went up according to custom. [...]
>
> After three days they found him in the temple, sitting among the teachers, listening to them and asking them questions.
>
> **And all who heard him were amazed at his understanding and his answers.** (Luke 2:41–42, 46–47 ESV)

It's not surprising that Jesus was a brilliant teacher. His teachings recorded by His disciples prove it beyond a doubt.

But it is surprising how early Jesus taught brilliantly. By 12 years old, before Jesus could shave, He could stun crowds.

This meant that during Jesus' childhood, He was an excellent student. Every Jewish child was trained in the Torah and the prophets at the local synagogue. But Jesus didn't learn it as a curiosity or a cultural duty. Jesus studied the Scriptures as though they were life itself.

Yet Jesus did this without sin. He possessed no arrogance or pride in His studies. He was gracious and kind even when He was the only one who knew the answer.

Jesus was normal, and Jesus was smart. What else defined His childhood?

Jesus had a big family.

Mary and Joseph raised many children beside Jesus. Mark 6:3 and Matthew 13:55–56 record that Jesus' brothers were James, Joses (or Joseph), Jude, and Simon. He had sisters, as well, who were mentioned but not by name.

That gives 5 male children and at least 2 female children. Jesus had no shortage of childhood playmates!

As the oldest male child, Jesus carried out many family responsibilities. He certainly played with his siblings, but He also helped raise them, as oldest children in big families often do by sheer necessity.

Jesus was normal, smart, and surrounded by siblings. What else can we glean?

Jesus was poor.

Mary and Joseph were not wealthy. They were about as far from wealthy as you can imagine. They were poor even by the standards of first-century peasants.

When Jesus was born, His parents presented Him to the Lord and offered a sacrifice as a the Law required.

Traditionally, this would be a lamb. But Leviticus 12:8 allowed those who were poor to bring an offering of two doves or two young pigeons instead, if they could not afford a lamb. This is the offering Mary and Joseph brought:

> Joseph and Mary⸎ brought Jesus⸎ up to Jerusalem⸎ to present him to the Lord (just as it is written in the law of the Lord, "Every firstborn male⸎ will be set apart to the Lord"⸎), and to offer a sacrifice according to what is specified in the law of the Lord, **a pair of doves⸎ or two young pigeons.**⸎ (Luke 2:22–24 NET)

Later on, the wise men from the east brought gifts of gold, frankincense, and myrrh. This made Jesus' family quite wealthy. But immediately an angel sent them away to Egypt to protect them from Herod, who sent soldiers to kill Jesus, whom Herod saw as a rival to the throne.

While they lived in Egypt, they lived on the wealth of these gifts. They returned to Israel after Herod died, but they returned to Nazareth and resumed their lives as peasants. Everyone in this village knew them as a normal family, as established above, so it's safe to assume the wealth of the gifts had been expended.

Even though Jesus was King, He lived as a peasant.

His adoptive father Joseph worked day-labor jobs, as would most carpenters and stone masons in Israel. Jesus and His brothers learned the family trade and joined in to help provide.

They did not live large; the average home in Israel at the time was around the size of a modern-day parking stall. This would have seemed normal to them, even with at least 9 people living inside.

What was Jesus like as a child?

- Normal.
- Smart.
- From a big family.
- Poor.

And from these beginnings, Jesus took less than four years to turn the world upside down. More people follow Him today than any other leader or religion. While countless people have described the death of Christianity, it continues to grow, reaching new countries, people groups, tribes, and languages every day.

We Christians really like our King.

He's God.

And yet He knows what it's like to be us.

Question 34

What are the biblical justifications for racial segregation?[49]

There are none — but there are a lot of people who thought there were.

First, establishing that the Bible gives no justification to segregation is easy. It's stated everywhere:

> There is neither Jew nor Greek, there is neither slave nor free, there is neither male nor female; **for you are all one in Christ Jesus.** (Galatians 3:28 ESV)

> For He Himself is our peace, who **has made the two one** and has **torn down the dividing wall of hostility.** (Ephesians 2:14 BSB)

> Here there is no Greek or Jew, circumcised or uncircumcised, barbarian, Scythian, slave, or free, but **Christ is all** and **is in all.** (Colossians 3:11 BSB)

Can you see how badly God wants to unite all of humanity as one in Jesus?

To see this even more clearly, consider the book of Philemon. The entire book is one letter from Paul to a man named Philemon, who once owned a slave named Onesimus.

In this letter, Paul has one main point: **stop seeing Onesimus as a slave and start seeing him as your equal**. I've quoted the main body of the letter below, so you can see for yourself:

> Accordingly, though I am bold enough in Christ to command you to do what is required, yet for love's sake I prefer to appeal to you—I, Paul, an old man and now a prisoner also for Christ Jesus— I appeal to you for my child, Onesimus, whose father I became in my imprisonment. (Formerly he was useless to you, but now he is indeed useful to you and to me.) I am sending him back to you, sending my very heart. I would have been glad to keep him with me, in order that he might serve me on your behalf during my imprisonment for the gospel, but I preferred to do nothing without your consent in order that your goodness might not be by compulsion but of your own accord. For this perhaps is why he was parted from you for a while, **that you might have him back forever, no longer as a bondservant but more than a bondservant, as a beloved brother**—especially to me, but how much more to you, both in the flesh and in the Lord.

> So if you consider me your partner, **receive him as you would receive me.** If he has wronged you at all, or owes you anything, charge that to my account. I, Paul, write this with my own hand: I will repay it—to say nothing of your owing me even your own self. Yes, brother, I want some benefit from you in the Lord. Refresh my heart in Christ. (Philemon 1:8–20 ESV)

Nothing in the Bible commands racial segregation. It's quite the opposite. **The Bible time and time again urges us to destroy segregation and become one.**

Question 35

Is there any archaeological proof that Jesus existed?[50]

YES.

There is more archaeological proof for Jesus' existence than for virtually any other figure from ancient history.

There's an abundance of corroborating archaeological evidence; a great amount of the people, cities, places, etc. of Jesus' life and ministry are established in the archaeological record. I'll summarize a lot of that at the end of this answer.

But when it comes to Jesus specifically, the best proof we have is the Bible.

Many people will object here. They will deny that the Bible can ever be used as proof of Jesus.

But this question doesn't get to make that objection. You asked for archaeological evidence of Jesus' existence, and the Bible fits the bill perfectly.

This wasn't always the case. Back when the King James Version was first translated from the Greek (roughly 400 years ago in 1611 A.D/C.E.), they had reference to perhaps a dozen Greek manuscripts of the New Testament. None of these were particularly old; they were removed from the time of Jesus by many hundreds, if not a thousand, years.

In such a situation, you could imagine all sorts of changes occurring in the text between the time it was first written to the time it was translated.

But then came archaeology.

In the last 150 years, archaeologists have dug up thousands of ancient biblical manuscripts. Today we have over 10,000 manuscripts of the New Testament in the original languages, stretching back in time to the early 2nd and late 1st centuries.

In all of this, *there is no evidence of the content changing over time.*

There are minor scribal issues, of course. There will always be minor copy issues when human agents perform the copying. But given the abundance of manuscripts, we can easily spot and correct these changes.

The evidence is so strong that even Bart Ehrman, one of the staunchest skeptics around, agrees. Out of the nearly 8,000 verses in the New Testament, Ehrman might quibble on perhaps a dozen, and none of these affect the teaching or beliefs of Christianity. They're all exceedingly minor issues. (For a complete interview with Ehrman on this subject, consult the appendix of Ehrman's book *Misquoting Jesus*).

What does all this have to do with archaeological proof for Jesus?

Everything.

Consider the impact of these three facts, all of which archaeology has established for the New Testament:

- It was written during the lifetimes of the eye-witnesses to Jesus.

- It was published in the lands where the events happened, while tens of thousands of eye-witnesses could put the lie to anything in them that wasn't accurate.

- It was not changed over time. The content of the New Testament today is the same as when it was first written.

All this happened during a time when Jesus' enemies held all the power and tried to destroy Christianity in any way possible. And yet they never charged the Bible with any kind of inaccuracy, nor did they attempt to argue that Jesus didn't exist.

Robert Van Voorst searched the first few centuries A.D./C.E and concluded clearly:

> "... [N]o pagans and Jews who opposed Christianity denied Jesus' historicity or even questioned it."[51]

He elaborates:

> "... [I]f anyone in the ancient world had a reason to dislike the Christian faith, it was the rabbis. To argue successfully that Jesus never existed but was a creation of early Christians would have been the most effective polemic against Christianity ... [Yet] all Jewish sources treated Jesus as a fully historical person ... [T]he rabbis ... **used the real events of Jesus' life against him**"[52]

Jesus' enemies unintentionally did Him a great service: they corroborated the accounts written about Him. They used the real events of Jesus' life against Him, which you only do when you cannot deny that those events happened.

To bring all this together:

Every hint of archaeology and history confirms what the New Testament says about Jesus.

To further establish the reliability of the New Testament accounts of Jesus, we can look to all of the background details. Do the places really exist as they're described? Did the people Jesus interacted with truly exist? Did they occupy the roles the Bible says they did? Did the culture behave as the Bible describes?

In all these cases, archaeology establishes a resounding *YES!*

On the <u>Sea of Galilee</u>, Christ's childhood town of Nazareth is still active today. In addition, ancient harbors matching the biblical record have been located in recent drought cycles. In fact, a first century <u>Galilean fishing boat</u> was recently unearthed from the mud and preserved. Although we have no idea who the boat belonged to, it matches the biblical record for the vessels used by Christ's disciples.

<u>Capernaum</u>, a town often visited by Jesus, is widely excavated and protected. Specific sites of interest include the <u>synagogue at Capernaum</u> where Jesus cured a man with an unclean spirit and delivered the sermon on the bread of life, and the <u>house of Peter</u> where Jesus healed Peter's mother-in-law and others.

Other archaeological sites involved in Christ's ministry include <u>Chorazin</u> (where Jesus taught in the synagogue), Kursi (the swine miracle), <u>Tabgha</u> (loaves and fishes), the Mount of Beatitudes (Sermon on the Mount), <u>Caesarea Philippi</u> (Peter's confession), and Jacob's well where Jesus spoke to the Samaritan woman.

In Jerusalem, we still see the foundations for the Jewish <u>Temple Mount</u> built by Herod the Great. Other remarkable sites in Jerusalem include the "Southern Steps" where Jesus and his followers entered the Temple, the <u>Pool of Bethesda</u> where Jesus healed a crippled man, and the recently uncovered Pool of Siloam where Jesus healed a blind man.

The evidence for Jesus in the events leading to his crucifixion starts across the Kidron Valley from Jerusalem at the Mount of Olives. There, we can walk through ancient olive trees to the Garden of Gethsemane where Jesus prayed before his capture. Then, we can look back across the Kidron Valley to the Golden Gate where Christ entered Jerusalem for his trial, scourging and death.

Elsewhere, we find more evidence for Jesus and the leaders presiding over his trial and crucifixion, including an inscription that mentions the Roman procurator of the time, Pontius Pilate, and the actual bones of the Jewish High Priest of the time, Caiaphas, preserved in an ornate ossuary (bone box). The evidence continues throughout Jerusalem where we can stand in the judgment place of Pontius Pilate called Gabbatha, and then walk the Via Dolorosa where Christ carried his own cross to Calvary. The huge Church of the Holy Sepulchre is considered by most scholars to be a reliable historical site covering the locations of the crucifixion and burial of Christ. Incredibly, a 2,000-year-old heel bone pierced by an iron nail was recently discovered in a Jerusalem graveyard that sheds more light on the practice of crucifixion by the first century Romans.[53]

Jerusalem from the Western Wall, similar to how it would appear in first-century Israel

I'll throw in one more tidbit, because this one's just fun:

In 64 A.D./C.E., Rome suffered a tragic fire. Nero blamed it on the Christians, to try to divert blame away from himself as the culprit.

Nero hated Christianity. But his hatred ended up serving Christianity. It provides a solid touchstone, historically.

Because of Nero, we know that within a mere 30 years after Jesus' death and Resurrection, Christianity had spread so far so rapidly that it had a sizable public presence in Rome.

Further, the historian who recorded the events, Tacitus, was one of the finest historians Rome ever produced. In his record, he corroborates several of the major facts about

Jesus. He also hated Christianity, yet his words still ended up serving the cause of Christ:

> [N]either human effort nor the emperor's generosity nor the placating of the gods ended the scandalous belief that the fire had been ordered [by Nero]. Therefore, to put down the rumor, Nero substituted as culprits and punished in the most unusual ways those hated for their shameful acts ... whom the crowd called "Chrestians." **The founder of this name, Christ [*Christus* in Latin], had been executed in the reign of Tiberius by the procurator Pontius Pilate** ... Suppressed for a time, the deadly superstition erupted again not only in Judea, the origin of this evil, but also in the city [Rome], where all things horrible and shameful from everywhere come together and become popular. (Tacitus, *Annals*, XV)

Touch points like these are critical because they destroy a great deal of silly arguments about Jesus. Some people erroneously claim that Paul invented the stories of Jesus, or that Paul took a humble peasant sage named Jesus and exaggerated the claims about Him to make his own religion.

But the 60's A.D./C.E. are when Paul wrote. By this time Christianity had already exploded in Judea and all over the Roman Empire.

It's simply impossible that Paul invented the stories about Jesus, because by the time he wrote, Christianity was already everywhere through the Empire.

Much more could be said, but to draw it to a conclusion:

The more we dig up, the more confirmation we find for everything the Bible says about Jesus.

Or to state it another way:

The more we dig up, it makes less and less sense to imagine that Jesus didn't exist, or that the stories about Him were wildly exaggerated. The evidence for such a thing simply doesn't exist.

Question 36

What, exactly, is your basis for believing that the Bible is true; not necessarily the word of God, but true?[54]

Let's break it down, starting with the end:

"not necessarily the word of God, but true?"

First and crucially: the Bible has to be the Word of God to be true. It cannot be true and not be the Word of God — because it claims directly to be the Word of God.

If the Bible is true, then it is the very words of God.

Next:

"What, exactly, is your basis for believing that the Bible is true?"

There are so many answers here I don't know where to begin. Let's list a few of them for starters:

- **Prophecy**. The Bible makes hundreds of claims about the future. So far, every single one has come true — *every single one*. Think about that. No other religion in the world dares to talk about the future as much as the Bible. There's a good reason for that: you only talk about the future in specific terms if you know specifically what's going to happen. If you make a guess and you're wrong, you've just tarnished your authority on the subject. **But God makes hundreds of prophecies about the future, and gets every one right. That's something only God can do.**

- **Accuracy.** No other book has been verified by archaeology as much as the Bible has. Some people try to argue this and point to one or two discoveries that might cast some down. But they miss two things: first, that *thousands* of discoveries have verified the major details all the way down to the tiniest intricacies, and second, that every discovery that "disproves" the Bible ends up disproved itself within about ten years. It's like clockwork.

- **Reliability.** You can trust what the Bible says about life. It describes humanity perfectly. Its wisdom is timeless. Its commands are the basis for every civilization that has come since. Its teachings aren't some pie-in-the-sky philosophy; it's tangible and practical and real, and if you build your life on it, you'll have an amazing life.

- **Consistency.** There are no contradictions in the Bible. **None.** People challenge this constantly and try to throw up a few examples. But each of these examples falls apart with about a 30 seconds of research. When people level their best attacks at the

Bible, yet it emerges unscathed, you begin to see how remarkable and unique this book truly is.

- **Power.** Jesus changes lives. Skeptics say that no one can change, that people are stuck in their ways. But I have witnessed Jesus transform lives time and time again. People with no hope for life discover a joy they can't contain. Wounded people find healing and peace for the first time in decades. Lost souls who drift from place to place find home for the first time ever, gaining a safety and trust they've never thought possible. Those who live to hurt people become those who live to heal others. It's simply amazing to watch the hopeless become the ambassadors of hope.

Those are the first five that came to mind. There are plenty more.

Question 37

What is the root cause of enmity between Islam, Christianity and Judaism?[55]

Jesus.

In Judaism, Jesus is a man who claimed to be Messiah (and, in their eyes, failed to be one).

In Islam, Jesus is a man Allah used as a prophet.

In Christianity, Jesus is God.

These claims cannot coexist.

If Jesus is just a man — even a man powerfully used by God — then Christianity is a lie.

If Jesus is God, then Islam is a lie and Judaism has rejected its truth.

This is why Jesus warned us that division would center around Him:

> "Do you think that I have come to give peace on earth? No, I tell you, but rather division." (Luke 12:51 ESV)

Jesus knew how polarizing He was. He left no room for gray areas.

As C. S. Lewis (and a few others) observed, if a man claims to be God, only four possibilities exist:

1. He is a liar, intentionally deceiving people.

2. He is a lunatic, absolutely crazy and worthy of being locked up.

3. He is a legend, someone who never claimed to be God but others said He did later.

4. He really is God.

Because of this, enmity is unavoidable.

Jesus knew this. Anyone who claims to be God is going to cause severe reactions.

But if Jesus really is God, and He wants to tell people, there's simply no way around this.

Enmity will happen. Jesus' name will cause division, more than any other, because there is no bigger question than who is God. The passion that people attach to their ideas of who God must be and their reactions to Jesus' claim will cause divisions unlike anything else the world has ever seen.

But if God is going to come into the world as a man, there simply is no other way.

Question 38

Is it accurate to say that humankind is "wired to worship"? Why is this the case and what does this mean?[56]

Look around you.

How many people are wearing clothes branded with their favorite sports team?

How many people use only Apple (or only Samsung, Microsoft, or Google) brand electronics?

How many people hang up posters of celebrities?

All of these are acts of worship.

Ask around you.

How many people have a favorite political party or candidate they'll tell you all about?

How many people keep singing the songs of their favorite musicians?

How many people can't wait to tell you about the latest book, TV show, or movie they really enjoyed?

All of these are acts of worship.

We are wired to worship.

When we find something extraordinary, we want to share it. We want to talk about it. We want others to experience it. We want others to affirm that what we love is truly amazing.

That's worship.

And if the object of worship is a person, then the heart of worship is to tell that person how amazing you think they are.

The curious piece is this: **the better the object of worship is, the more it satisfies you.**

If you worship a football team, it's going to be hard year if they keep getting beaten. But if the dominate, you're going to have an amazing time! You'll be filled with joy and your joy will radiate to others. When the thing you worship is the best around, if gives you matchless joy.

This is why God commands us to worship Him.

He is the perfection of everything good and praiseworthy. Beauty, majesty, wisdom, power, love, peace, dominion, knowledge — no one possesses or wields these better than God.

When we see this and we worship Him, we find joy that cannot he matched by anything else on this earth.

Many people believe in God but have never felt this way. When you ask them to describe God, you'll discover a curious thing: the God they describe is seldom worthy of worship at all.

Their problem is not that worship is boring. Their problem is that they do not see God clearly. And because they see a muted, corrupted shell of God, they find no joy in worshipping it.

We are wired to worship. We can't stop. We love finding amazing things and celebrating them.

And when you see God for the truth of who He is and you worship Him in His majesty, you will find the joy that all other worship envies.

Question 39

Why did God allow sin to enter this world?[57]

You could take this answer in a thousand different directions, but they all boil down to this: **sin entered the world because God gave authority to humanity.**

God could have created a race of robots who would only do His will. But He didn't want robots. He wanted children.

Further, God didn't want mindless slaves. God wanted children who would think, deliberate, create, act, and innovate. He created the Earth and gave it to humanity as our playground. He wants us to enjoy the wonders of Creation while contributing our own unique creations.

Take a look:

> Then God said, "Let us make man in our image, after our likeness. And **let them have dominion** over the fish of the sea and over the birds of the heavens and over the livestock and over all the earth and over every creeping thing that creeps on the earth."
>
> So God created man in his own image,
> in the image of God he created him;
> male and female he created them.

> And **God blessed them.** And God said to them, "Be fruitful and multiply and **fill the earth and subdue it**, and **have dominion** over the fish of the sea and over the birds of the heavens and over every living thing that moves on the earth." (Genesis 1:26–28 ESV)

God didn't want to micromanage humanity. He wanted to see what humanity could accomplish with an amazing world to care for and rule.

He carried this attitude from the beginning:

> Now out of the ground the LORD God had formed every beast of the field and every bird of the heavens and brought them to the man to see what he would call them. And **whatever the man called every living creature, that was its name.** The man gave names to all livestock and to the birds of the heavens and to every beast of the field. But for Adam there was not found a helper fit for him. (Genesis 2:19–20 ESV)

It would have been easy for God to tell the man what to call the animals. But that's not how God works. He wanted to give the man the freedom to be creative. Whatever the man wanted to call the animals, that was its name.

But what does all this have to do with sin? I'm glad you asked.

God gave humanity authority over the earth. That required the ability to make their own decisions.

For a while, the first two humans, Adam and Eve, chose to obey God. They did everything He asked and nothing He forbid. They used their creativity to take care of the Earth and all its inhabitants.

But then they decided to rebel against God. The serpent tempted them to rebel. But he did not control them. Eve and Adam chose to pursue their own desires and reject God's.

They sinned.

But they were not acting as mere individuals. They carried authority over the entire world. When they sinned, they allowed sin to creep into every corner of the earth: relationships and self-image and physical health and work and communication and trust and a million other things all became tarnished. Corruption began then.

At this point, God could have snapped His fingers and abolished sin from the earth. Except for the fact that He had given it to the care of humanity. To remove sin from the earth, He would have to remove the earth from the dominion of humanity. He would have to violate the very authority He had chosen to give.

Instead, **God continued to work within the authority structure He established.** He took on flesh and became a man — Jesus. **As a man, and therefore bearing the authority that God gave to humanity, Jesus went to the Cross.** He choose to die in the place of humanity to pay for all of our rebellions against God.

Jesus defeated sin. Its power to condemn us and separate us from God are broken. By following Jesus, we can overcome sin and begin regaining the lives God originally intended for us.

But humanity still retains the dominion God originally gave. Thus, we still have the choice of obeying sin or obeying God.

Why did God allow sin to enter the world? Because God gave the world to His children, and this is what we decided to do with it.

Question 40

Why is Jesus named Jesus?[58]

The answer is simple: **to prove that Jesus is both Savior and God.**

The Bible clearly states this in the following verse:

> "[Mary] will give birth to a son and you will name him Jesus, because he will save his people from their sins." (Matthew 1:21 NET)

The name Jesus means "Yahweh saves" or "Yahweh is salvation." It was a common name in Jesus' day. Certainly it did not mean that everyone named Jesus was God!

But look at what the angel said in the verse above. Why was Jesus given this specific name? *"Because He will save His people from their sins."*

Did you catch that?

Name this child "Yahweh saves," because He — this child — will save His people from their sins.

There's an immense amount of theology packed into those few words.

The angel did not say "Name him 'Yahweh saves,' because Yahweh will save." He said, "Name him 'Yahweh saves,' because *this child* will save."

If that wasn't clear enough, the next two verses make it even more explicit:

> This all happened so that what was spoken by the Lord through the prophet would be fulfilled: "Look! The virgin will conceive and bear a son, and they will call him Emmanuel," which means **"God with us."** (Matthew 1:22–23 NET)

Some people wonder how the name "Jesus" can fulfill a prophecy stating that they will call Him "Emmanuel." The reason is simple: both names establish clearly that the person who carries them is God.

He is called Jesus — "God saves" — because He will save.

He is called Emmanuel — "God with us" — because He is God dwelling with us.

Question 41

Do Christians and Jews know that we Muslims regard David & Jesus as equal with the Prophet Muhammad as prophets and messengers of God to mankind?[59]

Since the person who asked this question is a Muslim, I'll address my answer to Muslims.

Imagine that you are talking to someone about Islam. You are trying to tell them who Muhammad was. This person tells you they think Muhammad was smart, but wasn't a prophet.

You try to give them all the evidence. You quote the Qur'an. But no matter what you say, this person denies that Muhammad was a prophet. They genuinely believe he was smart and capable, but was just an ordinary person. They refuse to accept Muhammad as a prophet no matter what you say.

How does that make you feel? Angry? Frustrated? Sad that this person can't see the truth right in front of them? Mad that they're denigrating someone you cherish?

This is how Christians feel when you say that Jesus is merely a prophet.

Jesus did not claim to be a mere prophet. Jesus claimed to be God. When you say that you believe Jesus was a prophet, but only a prophet, we feel as offended as you feel when someone says Muhammad was a normal person, but not a prophet.

It sounds like absolute blasphemy to say that God can exist as a human being. God cannot have a son! God would never sleep with a human woman!

And here, we Christians actually agree with Muslims. God did not have a son. God did not sleep with a woman. God is far too Holy for that.

This is why Jesus did not claim to be the offspring of God. He did not claim to be a child created by God. He claimed to be God — directly.

The phrase "the Son of God" to the ancient Jews did not mean that Jesus was God's offspring. If that's what Jesus meant, He would have said that He was the "child of God," or something similar.

But "son" is a precise technical term, to the ancient Hebrew ear. It meant "the same as" or "one with."

You can see the word used this way throughout the entire Bible, but only one example needs to be made here:

> Again the high priest asked [Jesus], "Are you the Christ, **the Son of the Blessed?**" And Jesus said, "**I am**, and you will see the Son of Man seated at the right hand of Power, and coming with the clouds of heaven." (Mark 14:61–62 ESV).

The High Priest would not use the name of God, because he revered God too much. God is too Holy to use His name like a common man's. So he referred to God as "the Blessed."

By asking Jesus "Are you the Son of the Blessed" he directly asked "Are you claiming to be God?"

And Jesus said "**Yes**."

Again, it sounds like the worst blasphemy to say that God could be a human. This is exactly what the High Priest thought:

> And the high priest tore his garments and said, "What further witnesses do we need? **You have heard his blasphemy.** What is your decision?" And they all condemned him as deserving death. (Mark 14:63–64 ESV).

They clearly understood that Jesus claimed to be God — directly. That's why the High Priest had Him killed.

This was no distortion of facts. There is no evidence — none whatsoever — that this text was altered or changed throughout history. The earliest copies we have agree with this completely. **From the very beginning of Christianity, everyone understood that Jesus claimed to be God.**

To bring this back around:

Yes, Christians understand that Muslims regard David and Jesus as equal with the Prophet Muhammad as prophets and messengers of God to mankind.

That's why we reject Islam.

Jesus did not claim to be a mere prophet or messenger.

Jesus claimed to be God.

Question 42

How do you know that Jesus is merciful?[60]

Because He loves me and He saves me.

And I am the least deserving person on the planet.

Question 43

If Jesus had married and procreated children, could those children have sinned at any time?[61]

You don't have to punt this question to hypothetical children of Jesus.

Jesus could have sinned at any time.

That was one of the reasons He lived a full life in human flesh: to experience life as we do, complete with every kind of temptation to sin:

> We do not have a High Priest [Jesus] incapable of sympathizing with our weaknesses, but one **who has been tempted in every way just as we are**, yet without sin. (Hebrews 4:15 NET).

Some people think Jesus can't know what temptation is, since He never yielded to it. It's the opposite. None of the rest of us know how powerful temptation can be when it's ramped up to its fullest, because we have all yielded to it at lesser levels. **Jesus took the full force of temptation, every possible ounce of strength that temptation could level at Him, and He still resisted.**

It's not that Jesus was *unable* to sin.

Jesus was *unwilling* to sin.

Jesus knew that nothing good existed for Him outside of the will of God the Father. Jesus trusted this completely. Thus, whenever temptation offered something that seemed to be good but which was outside of the Father's will and plan, Jesus resisted the lie.

And it worked.

By avoiding sin, Jesus accomplished more in three and a half years than any human has ever been able to match.

Question 44

How are religions true?[62]

In the same way that anything else is true: it conforms to reality.

Religions get no free pass. If their claims don't describe reality, they're wrong and should be rejected. If the events and teachings described in their holy books didn't happen in real history, they're deceptive and should be rejected.

This is why Christianity stands alone. Its claims are all grounded in history, so much so that the earliest teachers of Christianity kept emphasizing that distinction. This is no pie-in-the-sky fairytale. This is real history — and that's why it matters.

Or as Paul said a short few years after Jesus died, was buried, and rose again:

> **If Christ has not been raised, then our preaching is in vain and your faith is in vain.** [...] But in fact Christ has been raised from the dead, the firstfruits of those who have fallen asleep. (1 Corinthians 15:14, 20 ESV).

But Paul knew people would need more evidence. So he gave them over 500 eye-witnesses to check with:

> For I delivered to you as of first importance what I also received: that **Christ died** for our sins in accordance with the Scriptures, that he was buried, that **he was raised on the third day** in accordance with the Scriptures, and that **he appeared to Cephas**, then to **the twelve.** Then he appeared to **more than five hundred brothers at one time**, most of whom are still alive, though some have fallen asleep. Then he appeared to **James**, then to **all the apostles.** Last of all, as to one untimely born, **he appeared also to me.** (1 Corinthians 15:3-8 ESV).

Why is Christianity true? For the same reason anything else is true: it conforms to reality. It really, truly happened.

Question 45

If in the Holy Bible there are contradictions that cannot be explained, what are they, and why are their explanations invalid?[63]

This is one of the most important questions about the Bible. If it contains contradictions that cannot be explained, it cannot be "Holy." After all, how could a book inspired by God get the facts wrong?

If the Bible is truly Holy, then every supposed contradiction will have a suitable explanation.

To be sure: there will *always* be claims of contradiction, simply because the Bible is thousands of years old and written from the viewpoint of a culture that is alien to most of us. There will be some differences in the way we think.

But — if the Bible is truly from God — then these supposed contradictions can all be explained away by looking at the history, the context, and the other details that shed light on the claims.

And I believe this is the case: **there are no contradictions in the Holy Bible. Every supposed contradiction**

possesses a clear explanation that wipes away the accusation.

Or to say it another way: **To clear up these contradictions, all you have to do is read the Bible.**

To demonstrate this, I'm going to rely on the structure provided in Timothy Morley's answer to "If in the Holy Bible there are contradictions that cannot be explained, what are they, and why are their explanations invalid?"[64] At the time of writing, it is the topmost answer to this question.

Timothy makes a good point: if the New Testament genuinely contains contradictions, then it cannot be the Word of God. He then provides ten examples of supposed contradictions, in an attempt to argue that the Scriptures are unreliable. **I'll take each in turn and provide the clear** explanation that removes the accusation of contradiction.

- *Contradiction #1: How did Judas Iscariot die?*
    - Matthew 27:5
        - Judas hung himself out of guilt.
    - Acts 1:18
        - Judas fell and "his body burst open".

The solution to this is easy: simply combine the details of the two accounts. They form one coherent story.

Why did Judas's body burst open when it fell? The answer is obvious: he hung himself and nobody cut him down for days. That's not a contradiction; those are two complementary details in a single story.

Acts 1:18 provides the context to understand this: "With the payment he received for his wickedness, Judas acquired a field; this was where he fell headlong, his body burst open and all his intestines spilled out."

Note that the test says Judas "acquired" this field; it does not use the normal verb for "bought." This is consistent with how you would speak if someone else (like the priests) bought the field using Judas' money and the populace continued to attribute the field to Judas after its purchase. The priests didn't use it for themselves; they used it for the one of the lowest possible uses (as they saw it): burial for foreigners. Since the priests didn't claim the field for their own use and the only ones to "use" it were deceased foreigners, the only prominent name to attach to the field was Judas'.

- ***Contradiction #2: Who was the father of Joseph, husband of Mary?***
  - Matthew 1:16
    - Joseph's father was Jacob.
  - Luke 3:23
    - Joseph's father was Heli.

This one again is easy. All you have to do is examine one verse:

> So Jesus, when He began His ministry, was about thirty years old. He was the son (as was supposed, of Joseph), the son of Heli. (Luke 3:23)

In other words: Jesus is the son (descendent) of Heli, Mary's father.

This is clearly seen in the Greek manuscripts. In the oldest copies we have, the ancestors of Jesus are set off in a column. Heli is the first name in these columns. Joseph's name is not in the column of ancestors. It only exists in the parenthetical comment by the author, which simply acknowledges that most people supposed Jesus to be

Joseph's son, even though Jesus was actually descended through Heli, who was Mary's father.

So again: there's no contradiction, here. It's very clearly a list of Mary's ancestors in Luke and Joseph's ancestors in Matthew.

- *Contradiction #3: Did Peter preach to Jews or Gentiles?*
    - Matthew 10:5–6
        - Peter (and all the disciples) were told to avoid Gentiles, and preach only to Jews.
    - Acts 15:7
        - Peter was told "some time ago" that he should preach to Gentiles.

This one, again, is easy. Matthew 10 occurs during Jesus' ministry when He focused on the nation of Israel. During the brief 3.5 years of Jesus' ministry, He focused almost exclusively on Israel, because He knew His time was short.

Acts 15 takes place years later when the game had shifted. Now the focus was to take Jesus' message to all the peoples of the world.

In short: Peter preached to both the Jews and the Gentiles. He began with the Jews, as Jesus told him to do, and expanded to the Gentiles after Jesus died, rose,

and ascended to Heaven. This is the story the book of Acts records.

Further, Acts 15:7 does not say "some time ago" to refer to the command Jesus gave a few years prior. The phrase literally says "**from ancient days.**" The point is that before the world began, God was already planning to carry the message of the Gospel to the whole world and knew who He would use to do it.

- *Contradiction #4: Are we saved by faith or works?*
  - Matthew 7:21
    - Faith is not enough; obedience to the Father is also necessary to enter heaven.
  - John 3:16
    - Anybody who believes in Christianity "shall not perish but have eternal life".

This one is — wait for it — easy.

"Believe" in the Bible never means "simply agree mentally that this is true." It *always* means "agree that this is true and live accordingly."

In other words, **it's impossible to believe in Christianity without obeying the Father.**

If you refuse to obey the Father, how can you believe He's truly God? If you truly believe that the Father is God — the all-powerful Creator of the universe who knows all truth and commands only good — then how can you refuse to obey Him? By refusing to obey you reveal that you don't truly believe He's God or has any authority over your life.

Or as Jesus says in Matthew 7:21, anyone can simply repeat the words. Anyone can say that Jesus is Lord. But how will you tell who really believes it and who is simply saying the words? You'll look at what they do. If they obey the Father, then they truly believe.

- ***Contradiction #5: Should good deeds be seen?***
    - Matthew 5:16
        - Good deeds should be seen.
    - Matthew 6:1–4
        - We must not "practice our righteousness in front others".

In order to kill the charge of contradiction here, all you have to do is quote the verses in full:

Matthew 5:16 "In the same way, let your light shine before others, **so that they** may see your good works and **give glory to your Father who is in heaven.**"

Matthew 6:1 "Beware of practicing your righteousness before other people **in order to be seen by them.**"

In other words: **The motives are being contrasted. Not the actions.**

There's not a hint of contradiction there.

- *Contradiction #6: According to Paul, is the law necessary or not?*
    - Romans 3:31
        - The law is to be upheld.
    - Romans 6:14
        - Christians are no longer under the law, but "under grace".

Again, simply read the flow of thought in Romans and this charge of contradiction evaporates.

In Romans 3:31, Paul isn't talking about a law of works. He's talking about faith — about simply believing the Gospel of Jesus Christ. Look:

> Then what becomes of our boasting? It is excluded. **By what kind of law? By a law of works? No, but by the law of faith.** For we hold that one is justified by faith apart from works of the law. Or is God the God of Jews only? Is he not the God of Gentiles also? Yes, of Gentiles also, since God is one—who will justify the circumcised by faith and the uncircumcised through faith. **Do we then overthrow the law by this faith? By no**

> **means! On the contrary, we uphold the law.** (Romans 3:27-31)

In other words: we uphold the law — **by believing.** Not by being slaves to obeying a system of rules.

How did we go from a system of obeying rules to a system of believing? **By grace:**

> Therefore, since we have been justified by faith, we have peace with God through our Lord Jesus Christ. Through him we have also obtained access **by faith into this grace** in which we stand, and we rejoice in hope of the glory of God. (Romans 5:1-2).

By upholding the law of faith — by believing — we enter into grace, instead of being bound by the law of rules. Thus:

> For sin will have no dominion over you, **since you are not under law but under grace.** (Romans 6:14)

The flow of thought is clear. It only appears to be a contradiction when you cherry-pick certain phrases out of context and try to make them sound contradictory.

- *Contradiction #7: How many believers were there at the time of the ascension?*
    - Acts 1:15
        - There were about 120 believers.

- 1 Corinthians 15:6

    - There were more than 500 believers.

This one might be the easiest. **The counts reflect different events.**

In 1 Corinthians 15:6, Paul refers to the 500 who saw Jesus ascend into Heaven.

Acts 1:15 takes place **9 days later**, when a smaller group were gathered together in an upper room. Only 120 were present at this time. We don't know why the number is less; maybe the room only held 120, or the rest had left in the 9 days since the Ascension to their homes elsewhere.

In any case, it's not a contradiction to say that 500 people gathered together at one place, then 9 days later 120 of them gathered at a different place.

- *Contradiction #9: Is righteousness possible, and can it lead to salvation?*

    - Matthew 25:46

        - The righteous will have eternal life.

    - Romans 3:10

        - There is "no one righteous, not even one".

Again: follow the flow of thought and the contradiction disappears.

Matthew 25 discusses **righteous behavior — doing the right things.**

Romans 3:10 discusses how **no one starts out seeking God.**

The topics are completely different subjects! But because they use one similar word, they're charged with contradiction.

Look at the full phrase from Romans 3:9–11:

> What then? Are we Jews any better off? No, not at all. For we have already charged that all, both Jews and Greeks, are under sin, as it is written: "**None is righteous, no, not one; no one understands; no one seeks for God**. (Romans 3:9-11).

Is Romans trying to say that no one on earth actually seeks God? Of course not! He's stating that everyone — Jews and Greeks — starts out apart from God. No one starts out in a better place than someone else.

Contrast this with Matthew 25, where Jesus is saying that those who don't take care of those in need are demonstrating that they don't believe or God. Those who do care for those in need demonstrate that they do believe and obey God, and those are the ones who have been saved.

These are completely different topics! There's no contradiction — only a similar word used twice.

- *Contradiction #10: When did Jesus (peace be upon him) ascend?*
    - Luke 24:21
        - The third day after the crucifixion
    - Acts 1:3
        - Jesus (peace be upon him) remained among the disciples for forty days.

This one clears up easily. **Luke 24:21 does not say that Jesus ascended 3 days after the Crucifixion. Luke 24:21 doesn't say anything about the Ascension at all!**

In Luke 24, Jesus is talking with two disciples walking along the road to Emaus. They don't realize they're speaking to Jesus, so they begin telling Him about all that had happened. In so doing, they mention that Jesus' death happened three days prior.

That's where the 3 days comes from.

Now here's the slight bit of confusion: the text breaks twice between then and the end of Luke 24. After verse 43 and after verse 49 the text breaks, indicating that the scene has ended and a new one begins in the next verse.

This wouldn't be so confusing, except that several translation (such as the NIV, which is used in the supposed contradiction charge above) insert the word "Then" at the beginning of each of these next two scenes.

The word "then" is not in the text. The word used is "And," indicating simply that another scene is being told. But in modern English it's bad form to begin a new paragraph with "And," so "Then" is used in its place. This causes people to think that each new scene follows immediately from the last — but that's not what the text indicates.

Thus, many readers today miss these breaks and assume it all happens on the same day. It does not.

How can we know for sure? Because it's impossible for Luke 24:21 and Luke 24:50 to happen on the same day. In Luke 24:29 it is "near evening," and this is before the two disciples run all the miles back to Jerusalem. By the time they gather with the rest of the group in Luke 24:33, it is fully night.

In other words — it's completely dark outside.

How could Jesus lead a huge crowd out to a mountain in Luke 24:50 and ascend? They wouldn't be able to see Him! Remember that this is a day and age with no electric lighting. When the sun goes down at night, you go down, because there isn't enough artificial light to see anything outside.

At the very least, then, we can see that Luke 24:50 cannot happen on the same day as Luke 24:21. Since Luke, the author, does not specify how many days apart the last few scenes are, we can only guess. Thankfully, Luke writes another book, called Acts. In this, he clarifies the length of time: 40 days precisely.

This answer was long, but necessary.

None of these supposed "contradictions" holds weight when you scratch beneath the surface.

The Holy Bible is the most studied book in all of human history. It is the best-selling book of all time. More people read it and study it every day than anything else.

Every supposed contradiction has been examined countless times. None have held up.

Question 46

Why is Esther in the Bible when it doesn't mention God?[65]

Esther exists in the Bible to demonstrate that God is fully capable of protecting his people through the hidden hand of **Providence**, just as well as He can through the visible hand of **Miracles**.

The books of Esther and Daniel are back to back, chronologically. But while Daniel is chock full of miracles, Esther is devoid of them.

Why are they so different if they're from the same time period, the same ethnic group, in the same region of the world?

Because they're demonstrating two different scenarios.

In Daniel, God demonstrates that He is capable and willing to intercede for His people through visible supernatural means. This happens through dreams, visions, and outright miracles.

In Esther, God demonstrates that He is capable and willing to intercede for His people through hidden "natural" means. This happens through a king having a sleepless night, a woman being in exactly the right place at the right time, a man being exactly in the right place to overhear secrets, etc.

In both, God defends and protects His people. In both, human agents have real choices to make and responsibilities to bear. In both, God directs events to preserve His children and glorify His Name.

Both books reveal God. They reveal two different strategies for how God works.

Question 47

How did slave owners justify slavery using the Bible?[66]

By ignoring what the Bible actually says and twisting it into an abomination of itself.

Slave owners twisted concepts like the mark of Cain or the curse of Ham to justify slavery. I'll explain those in a second.

But the bigger issue is this: slave owners saw the word "slave" in the Bible and assumed it referred to what they were doing. It did not.

The Bible explicitly destroys the abuses of slavery and rebuilds a system of respect-driven employment in its place. But because it keeps using the word "slave," those who want to abuse others ignored the Bible's new system of respect and used the mere word "slave" to justify their abuses.

First, let's explore two of the most popular justifications for slavery, the mark of Cain and the curse of Ham. As John Perkins explains:

> Over the years some church leaders have used stories such as the mark of Cain in Genesis 4:1–17 and the curse of Ham in Genesis 9:20–27 to justify

the separation of people based on skin color, as well as their supremacist views. In these wrong, and racially motivated interpretations, God punished Cain for murdering Abel by exiling him to the land of Nod, and later God cursed the offspring of Noah's son Ham, who became the forefather of many African nations. Neither of these readings holds much water. There's nothing in the text, for instance, that describes the physical form of Cain's mark or that suggests it was something passed down through his descendants. In addition, the "mark" itself was not placed on Cain to make him a target for oppression, as some racist scholars have taught, but to make it clear (in God's mercy) that no one else should seek to harm Cain. Likewise, Noah's curse on Ham is not described in detail, In fact, it appears this "curse" was placed on Ham's son Canaan, not Ham or his other sons. Also, the curse seems to be fulfilled when the children of Israel take possession of the land of Canaan (see Josh. 21:43). So, the once-popular idea among some Christians that the black race is inferior and deserving of being enslaved because of a divine curse does not hold up under examination.[67]

Second, let's explore what the Bible actually commands.

Some people take verses like "Slaves, obey your masters" (1 Peter 2:18) and try to claim that it justifies slavery. It does not, because the word "slave" to them did not mean what "slave" meant in the American south.

In the Old Testament, God redefined every aspect of slavery to transform it into the world's first respect-driven system of employment. **Slaves were literally employees.** They could walk away from any master who abused them, just as any employee today can walk away from any boss who abused them.

Check the source:

> **You must not return an escaped slave to his master** when he has run away to you. Indeed, he may live among you in any place he chooses, in whichever of your villages he prefers; **you must not oppress him.** (Deuteronomy 23:15-16 NET)

In other words: if a slave ever leaves his master, the master is forbidden from getting that slave back. Each slave is as free to leave his master as a modern-day employee is to walk out the doors of a bad work situation.

Further, wherever that former slave decides to live now, the residents there cannot oppress him. They must respect him and let him live among them. They will not stuffed into ghettos or abandoned into the wilderness; the Law protects their ability to live wherever they choose.

Do you see the respect given to every "slave" in the Bible? **They have all the power!** If the master abuses them, they can simply walk away, stripping that master of any economic power. Wherever that former slave goes, he or she is to be welcomed as a fellow citizen, honored, and allowed to live peacefully wherever they like.

God bends over backwards to remove abuse and restore honor. Consider these further examples:

- Slavery was not permanent in Israel. Slaves were released every seven years. (Exodus 21:2).

- Slaves could not be killed, and when a master did kill a slave, the master was punished for taking a human life. (Exodus 21:20).

- Slaves had a mandatory day of rest every week, just like everyone else. (Exodus 20:10).

- Slaves were to be treated as hired workers who will be released in a few years, not as human property. (Leviticus 25:39-43).

- If a master permanently injured a slave, that slave was immediately set free. The permanent injury could be as small as knocking out a tooth. (Exodus 21:26-27).

Thus I repeat: How did slave owners justify slavery using the Bible?

By ignoring what the Bible actually says and twisting it into an abomination of itself.

If you treat people as the Bible commands, you will never abuse another person.

Question 48

If God made it easy to believe in Him, would everyone do it?[68]

The answer is simple: **No.**

The problem has never been God failing to reveal Himself. **The problem is that even when God reveals Himself clearly, some people still refuse to believe.**

Jesus experienced this constantly. One of the most dramatic times occurs here:

> Then a demon-oppressed man who was blind and mute was brought to him, and Jesus healed him, so that the man spoke and saw. And all the people were amazed, and said, "Can this be the Son of David?" But when the Pharisees heard it, they said, "It is only by Beelzebul, the prince of demons, that this man casts out demons." (Matthew 12:22–24 ESV)

The evidence could not be clearer. Jesus claims to be God, then does what only God can do: casting out demons and restoring sight and speech to a man blind and deaf.

The crowds understood what the miracles meant. If Jesus claims to be God and does what only God can do, then the conclusion is unavoidable: Jesus is God.

But many Pharisees refused this idea. They had already decided to reject Jesus, regardless of the evidence. So they invented a ridiculous counter-explanation: Jesus only casts out demons by the power of other demons.

The point is clear: **Jesus can stare you in the face and perform miracles abundantly. But those who have already determined to reject Jesus will continue to reject Him, no matter how clear the evidence.**

Jesus made it abundantly easy to believe Him. As a result, a great many did. The number of people who believe in Jesus today is currently around 3 billion, growing steadily since Jesus made His claims 2,000 years ago.

But there will always be those who decide to reject Jesus. You can make the path to belief in Jesus as easy and obvious as possible – and they will still turn away.

More than anything else in life, this breaks my heart.

Afterward

Let me leave you with one thought: *never stop asking.*

As Christians, we serve an infinite God. He possesses all wisdom, all knowledge, and all cleverness. He has every answer to every question. He fears no truth and hides from no challenge.

This does not mean every answer is easy. Jesus often answered clear questions with cryptic parables or riddles. The truth was present, but it took work to brush away the dirt and find the nuggets of gold.

Some people hold back from asking. They avoid questions with phrases like "God works in mysterious ways," or "Faith can't have certainty, or else it's not faith."

That's not how God works.

God filled a massive Bible with clear words direct from His Voice and His Spirit. God took on flesh as a clear Person in Jesus Christ, showing us exactly who God is.

God is glorified in truth — both its search and its revelation. As the Word of God testifies, "It is the glory of God to conceal a matter, but to search out a matter is the glory of kings" (Proverbs 25:2).

So search it out.

Take your questions, everything pressing on your mind, anything that you want to know. Bring it before God. Ask Him to reveal the truth.

God has already given you a head start. The truths contained in the Scriptures tackle every area of life and give you the surest footing you could ever hope to have. Every single word in the Scriptures is true.

God has also filled you with His Holy Spirit, whom Jesus describes as your revealer of truth: "the Helper, the Holy Spirit, whom the Father will send in My name, *He will teach you all things* and bring to your remembrance all that I have said to you" (John 14:26).

Our God has no limits. His wisdom is eternal. And He is always ready to help: "If any of you lacks wisdom, let him ask God, who gives generously to all without reproach, and it will be given" (James 1:5).

Ask. God's ears are open. And He is already speaking.

I hope you're curious.

Endnotes

[1] Thomas, David. Comment written in response to Kyle Davison Bair's answer to "What is the best evidence for a historical Jesus?" *Quora*, 5 Jan. 2014, https://www.quora.com/What-is-the-best-evidence-for-a-historical-Jesus

[2] Henderson, James. Comment written in response to Kyle Davison Bair's answer to "If in the Holy Bible there are contradictions that cannot be explained, what are they, and why are their explanations invalid?" *Quora*, 22 Oct. 2015, https://www.quora.com/If-in-the-Holy-Bible-there-are-contradictions-that-cannot-be-explained-what-are-they-Are-their-explanations-invalid

[3] Mermikli, Janice. Comment written in response to Kyle Davison Bair's answer to "What evidence is there for Jesus Christ's death, burial, and resurrection?" *Quora*, 17 May 2011, https://www.quora.com/What-evidence-is-there-for-Jesus-Christs-death-burial-and-resurrection

[4] Lamping, Daniel. Comment written in response to Kyle Davison Bair's answer to "What is the best evidence for a historical Jesus?" *Quora*, 5 Jan. 2014, https://www.quora.com/What-is-the-best-evidence-for-a-historical-Jesus

[5] Merchant, Mustafa. "Which religion is the true religion & why?" *Quora*, 24 December 2015, https://www.quora.com/Which-religion-is-the-true-religion-why

[6] Arnold, Thomas. *Christian Life, Its Hopes, Its Fears, and Its Close*, 6th ed. (London: T. Fellowes, 1859), pp. 14-16.

[7] "Do You Believe That the Tree of Knowledge of Good and Bad Was Meant to Be Eaten from? Do You Feel That Perhaps a Certain Time Would Have ..." *Quora*, 11 July 2014, https://www.quora.com/Do-you-believe-that-the-Tree-of-Knowledge-of-Good-and-Bad-was-meant-to-be-eaten-from-Do-you-feel-that-perhaps-a-certain-time-would-have-to-pass-gaining-experience-as-sinners-before-God-would-allow-the-tree-to-be-eaten-from

[8] STEMsolver. "Suppose If God Existed Then X, and If God Didn't Exist Then Y. What Do You Think Are X and Y?" *Quora*, 7 Jan. 2020, https://www.quora.com/Suppose-if-God-existed-then-X-and-if-God-didnt-exist-then-Y-What-do-you-think-are-X-and-Y

[9] See, Austin. "When Will the Star of Bethlehem Be Visible Again?" *Quora*, 30 June 2015, https://www.quora.com/When-will-the-star-of-Bethlehem-be-visible-again

[10] This screencap has been modified from originals produced by Rick Larson

for the documentary "The Star of Bethlehem." They were captured from https://www.youtube.com/watch?v=exmbuX1NffU To purchase the documentary, visit bethlehemstar.net.

[11] Diaz, Linda. "The Shepherd Is a Prominent, Meaningful Metaphor in the Bible. But Why Do the Prophets Ask Us to Think of Messiah as Our Good Shepherd?" *Quora*, 25 Dec. 2019, https://www.quora.com/q/heojwpvafuraiuio/The-shepherd-is-a-prominent-meaningful-metaphor-in-the-Bible-But-why-do-the-prophets-ask-us-to-think-of-Messiah-as-our

[12] Parson, Chris. "What Is the Hardest Thing to Believe in the Bible?" *Quora*, 22 Dec. 2019, https://www.quora.com/What-is-the-hardest-thing-to-believe-in-the-Bible

[13] Bloemers, Marc. "Is It True That Many Christians Believe That Both Heaven and Hell Are a State of Mind Rather than an Actual Place?" *Quora*, 22 Dec. 2019, https://www.quora.com/Is-it-true-that-many-Christians-believe-that-both-heaven-and-hell-are-a-state-of-mind-rather-than-an-actual-place

[14] Foo-Chong Soo'ialo, Peti. "Why and How Should I Read the Bible?" *Quora*, 25 Aug. 2012, https://www.quora.com/Why-and-how-should-I-read-the-bible

[15] Cole, Arnold, Ed.D, and Ovwigho, Pamela Caudill, PhD. (2009). Understanding the Bible Engagement Challenge: Scientific Evidence for the Power of 4. [ebook] Center for Biblical Engagement. Available at: https://bttbfiles.com/web/docs/cbe/Scientific_Evidence_for_the_Power_of_4.pdf [Accessed 27 Jan. 2020].

[16] "How Can Anyone Explain the Trinity in Simple Language? I Have Been Struggling with It for over 20 Years and No Priest Was Able to Give a ..." *Quora*, 25 Nov. 2019, https://www.quora.com/How-can-anyone-explain-the-Trinity-in-simple-language-I-have-been-struggling-with-it-for-over-20-years-and-no-priest-was-able-to-give-a-convincing-explanation

[17] Balazs, Jason. "How Do I Grow My Faith in Christianity?" *Quora*, 31 Jan. 2019, https://www.quora.com/How-do-I-grow-my-faith-in-Christianity-I-m-still-young-and-have-big-dreams-and-aspirations-but-want-to-achieve-them-the-right-way-in-gods-word-I-have-good-days-and-praise-him-a-lot-but-when-the-days-going-bad-I

[18] Sander, Nathan. "Unlike Other Failed Messiahs, Why Did Jesus' Message/Sect Endure after His Death?" *Quora*, 15 Nov. 2019, https://www.quora.com/Unlike-other-failed-Messiahs-why-did-Jesus-message-sect-endure-after-his-death

[19] "Do You Find It Incomprehensible That despite the Track Record of Science in Improving People's Lives, Evangelicals Will Still Give Greate..." *Quora*, 12 Nov. 2019, https://www.quora.com/Do-you-find-it-incomprehensible-that-despite-the-track-record-of-science-in-improving-people-s-lives-evangelicals-will-still-give-greater-credence-to-blind-acceptance-of-scripture

[20] *34 Great Scientists Who Were Committed Christians*. [online] Famousscientists.org. Available at: https://www.famousscientists.org/great-scientists-christians/ [Accessed 27 Jan. 2020].

[21] Rachul, Finnlay. "What Parts of the New Testament Have Been Significantly Edited?" *Quora*, 10 Nov. 2019, https://www.quora.com/What-parts-of-the-New-Testament-have-been-significantly-edited

[22] Vitols, Paul. "What Is the Origin of the Idea of a Loving God?" *Quora*, 6 Nov. 2019, https://www.quora.com/What-is-the-origin-of-the-idea-of-a-loving-God

[23] Perttu, Torbjörn. "Why Were the Four Canonical Gospels Written so Long after Christ's Death and Resurrection?" *Quora*, 1 Mar. 2014, https://www.quora.com/Why-were-the-four-canonical-gospels-written-so-long-after-Christs-death-and-resurrection

[24] Sotiropoulos, Dimitris. "Is not most unfair to Jesus that three main branches of Christianity claim to derive their divine mandate from Him as God, although He said: "Why callest thou me good, none is good except the Father" and 'Why hast thou forsaken me,my God, my God?'" *Quora*, 16 Oct. 2019, https://www.quora.com/Isnt-it-most-unfair-to-Jesus-that-the-three-main-branches-of-Christianity-claim-to-derive-their-divine-mandate-from-Him-as-God-although-He-said-Why-callest-thou-me-good-none-is-good-except-the-Father

[25] Manson, Ray. "Why did God punish Eve harder than Adam when he only told Adam not to eat the Apple?" *Quora*, 3 Nov. 2018, https://www.quora.com/Why-did-God-punish-Eve-harder-than-Adam-when-he-only-told-Adam-not-to-eat-the-Apple

[26] Thiagarajan, Samuel Dharmaraj. "How does the Christian belief in the resurrection provide a resource for dealing with and understanding suffering?" *Quora*, 8 Sep. 2019, https://www.quora.com/q/giojtzcmrpbtlecd/How-does-the-Christian-belief-in-the-resurrection-provide-a-resource-for-dealing-with-and-understanding-suffering

[27] Chandran, Ramesh. "Was there an eclipse when Jesus was crucified?" *Quora*, 12 Jun. 2019, https://www.quora.com/Was-there-an-eclipse-when-Jesus-was-crucified

[28] Psaila, Shaun. "What causes involuntary neurons to fire in a random way that creates thoughts that we are opposed to thinking? Could the devil be involved in having deceptive messages and past conditioning?" *Quora*, 10 Jul 2019, https://www.quora.com/What-causes-involuntary-neurons-to-fire-in-a-random-way-that-creates-thoughts-that-we-are-opposed-to-thinking-Could-the-devil-be-involved-in-having-deceptive-messages-and-past-conditioning

[29] Text quoted from the description listed on *Christ-Centered Therapy's* Amazon page: https://www.amazon.com/Christ-Centered-Therapy-Neil-T-Anderson/dp/0310231132/ref=sr_1_1?keywords=christ-centered+therapy&qid=1580862854&sr=8-1 [Accessed 4 February 2020].

[30] Psaila, Shaun. "How do we know how the apostles died is there evidence?" *Quora*, 15 Jul 2019, https://www.quora.com/How-do-we-know-how-the-apostles-died-Is-there-evidence

[31] McDowell, Sean. "A Historical Evaluation of the Evidence for the Death of the Apostles as Martyrs for Their Faith." *Southern Baptist Theological Seminary*. December 2014, https://digital.library.sbts.edu/handle/10392/4857

[32] Ibid, 424-428.

[33] Miller, Zoya. "Do the majority of Christians believe that you can't be a good person without being a Christian?" *Quora*, 18 Mar. 2019, https://www.quora.com/Do-the-majority-of-Christians-believe-that-you-can-t-be-a-good-person-without-being-a-Christian

[34] Austin, Tad. "Why do the Gospels differ in Jesus' response to the High Priest when asked if he is the Messiah? He either answers cryptically or in the affirmative." *Quora*, 11 Mar. 2019, https://www.quora.com/Why-do-the-Gospels-differ-in-Jesus-response-to-the-High-Priest-when-asked-if-he-is-the-Messiah-He-either-answers-cryptically-or-in-the-affirmative

[35] Cheney, Johnston M., and Ellisen, Stanley A., *Jesus Christ The Greatest Life: A Unique Blending of the Four Gospels* (Eugene, OR: Paradise Publishing Inc., 1999), 240–250.

[36] Adkins, Hazel. "Sarah Sanders has stated her belief that God wanted Trump to be president. Do you agree? If so, why do you think this is so?" *Quora*, 31 Jan. 2019, https://www.quora.com/Do-you-agree-with-Sarah-Sanders-belief-that-God-wanted-Trump-to-be-president-Why-do-you-think-this-is-so

[37] Reaper, Gerard. "Do Christians mind being friends with people who hate everything about Christianity?" *Quora*, 31 Jan 2019, https://www.quora.com/Do-Christians-mind-being-friends-with-people-who-hate-everything-about-Christianity

[38] Kaufman, Mordechai. "What would Jesus say about Christianity today?" *Quora*, 30 Apr 2019, https://www.quora.com/What-would-Jesus-say-about-Christianity-today

[39] Dutta, Nihal. "What are some of the best ways to say 'I love you' without actually saying it?" *Quora*, 16 Jan 2016, https://www.quora.com/What-are-some-of-the-best-ways-to-express-I-love-you-without-actually-saying-it

[40] Donkor, Grace. "Who is Jesus, God or the Son of God?" *Quora*, 9 Oct 2014, https://www.quora.com/Who-is-Jesus-God-or-the-Son-of-God

[41] Parks, Jay. "What evidence is there for Jesus Christ's death, burial, and resurrection?" *Quora*, 17 May 2011, https://www.quora.com/What-evidence-is-there-for-Jesus-Christs-death-burial-and-resurrection

[42] Craig, William Lane. "The Evidence for Jesus." *Reasonable Faith*, https://www.reasonablefaith.org/writings/popular-writings/jesus-of-nazareth/the-evidence-for-jesus. [Accessed on 4 February 2020].

[43] Ibid.

[44] Lee, Harris. "If God's plan had allowed millions of Jews to die in holocaust, does God kill people he hates by disease and accident?" *Quora*, 4 Jan 2019, https://www.quora.com/If-Gods-plan-had-allowed-millions-of-Jews-to-die-in-the-Holocaust-does-God-kill-people-he-hate-by-diseases-and-accidents

[45] Lewiston, David. "How would a skilled magician / prestidigitator perform the alleged miracles of Jesus, only using technology available at the time?" *Quora*, 1 Jan 2019, https://www.quora.com/How-would-a-skilled-magician-prestidigitator-perform-some-of-the-alleged-miracles-of-Jesus-only-using-the-technology-available-at-the-time

[46] "Why are the Greek gods considered myths while Christianity isn't? edit." *Quora*, 25 Nov. 2016, https://www.quora.com/Why-are-the-Greek-gods-considered-myths-while-the-Christian-god-isn%E2%80%99t

[47] "Religious Affiliation and Suicide Attempt," Kanita Dervic, Maria A. Oquendo, Michael F. Grunebaum, Steve Ellis, Ainsley K. Burke, and J. John Mann. American Journal of Psychiatry, 2004.

[48] Taylor, Bruce. "Do you ever wonder about the details of Jesus' childhood?" *Quora*, 24 Dec. 2019, https://www.quora.com/Do-you-ever-speculate-about-the-details-of-Jesus-childhood

[49] Gurning, Hotdin. "What are the biblical justifications for racial segregation?" *Quora*, 12 Dec. 2018, https://www.quora.com/What-are-the-biblical-justifications-for-racial-segregation

[50] "What is the best evidence for a historical Jesus?" *Quora*, 5 Jan. 2014, https://www.quora.com/What-is-the-best-evidence-for-a-historical-Jesus

[51] Van Voorst, Robert. *Jesus Outside*. (Grand Rapids: Eerdmans, 2000), p. 15.

[52] Ibid, 133-134.

[53] *Evidence For Jesus*. [online] Available at: https://www.allaboutarchaeology.org/evidence-for-jesus.htm [Accessed 27 Jan. 2020].

[54] Khan, Aazam. "What, exactly, is your basis for believing that the Bible is True; not necessarily the word of god, but true?" *Quora*, 7 Dec. 2018, https://www.quora.com/What-exactly-is-your-basis-for-believing-that-the-Bible-is-True-not-necessarily-the-word-of-god-but-true

[55] Mohaisen, David. "What is the root cause of enmity between Islam, Christianity and Judaism?" *Quora*, 5 Dec. 2018, https://www.quora.com/What-is-the-root-cause-of-enmity-between-Islam-Christianity-and-Judaism

[56] Williams, Nate. "Is it accurate to say that humankind is 'wired to worship'? Why is this the case and what does this mean?" *Quora*, 2 Dec. 2018, https://www.quora.com/Is-it-accurate-to-say-that-humankind-is-wired-to-worship-Why-is-this-the-case-and-what-does-this-mean

[57] "What is the reason God allowed sin to enter this world?" *Quora*, 9 Jul. 2014, https://www.quora.com/What-is-the-reason-God-allowed-sin-to-enter-this-world

[58] Cayona, Jared. "Why is jesus named jesus?" *Quora*, 29 Sep. 2015, https://www.quora.com/Why-is-Jesus-named-Jesus

[59] Katsina, Misbahu Naiya. "Do Christians and Jews know that we Muslims regard David & Jesus as EQUAL with Prophet Muhammad as Prophets and Messengers of God to mankind?" *Quora*, 15 Nov. 2018, https://www.quora.com/Do-Christians-and-Jews-know-that-we-Muslims-

regard-David-Jesus-as-equal-with-the-Prophet-Muhammad-as-prophets-and-messengers-of-God-to-mankind

[60] Leeper, Greg. "How do you know that Jesus is merciful?" *Quora*, 18 Nov. 2018, https://www.quora.com/How-do-you-know-that-Jesus-is-merciful

[61] Smith, Augustus. "(Assuredly) Jesus was asexual given that his whole mission was spiritually based; (Provokably) If Jesus has married and had children; (Disputably) would / could those children have sinned at any time?" *Quora*, 18 Nov. 2018, https://www.quora.com/Jesus-was-asexual-given-that-his-whole-mission-was-spiritually-based-If-Jesus-had-married-and-procreated-children-would-could-those-children-have-sinned-at-any-time

[62] "How are religions true?" *Quora*, 14 Nov. 2018, https://www.quora.com/How-are-religions-true

[63] "If there are, in fact, contradictions in the scriptures that cannot be explained, what are they, and why are their explanations invalid?" *Quora*, 22 Oct. 2015, https://www.quora.com/If-in-the-Holy-Bible-there-are-contradictions-that-cannot-be-explained-what-are-they-Are-their-explanations-invalid

[64] Morley, Timothy. *Timothy Morley's answer to "If in the Holy Bible there are contradictions that cannot be explained, what are they? Are their explanations invalid?" - Quora.* [online] Available at: https://qr.ae/TUhUvf [Accessed 27 Jan. 2020].

[65] Hector, Ewan. "Why is Esther in the Bible when it doesn't mention God?" *Quora*, 4 Nov. 2018, https://www.quora.com/Why-is-Esther-in-the-Bible-when-it-doesnt-mention-God

[66] "How did slave owners justify slavery using the Bible?" *Quora*, 3 Nov. 2018, https://www.quora.com/How-did-slave-owners-justify-slavery-using-the-Bible-1

[67] Perkins, John. *One Blood: Parting Words to the Church on Race.* (Chicago: Moody Publishers, 2018), p.49.

[68] Brodski, James. "If God Made It Easy to Believe in Him, Would Everyone Do It?" *Quora*, 4 Jan. 2020, https://www.quora.com/If-God-made-it-easy-to-believe-in-him-would-everyone-do-it

Made in the USA
Monee, IL
21 February 2020